At Issue

What Motivates Suicide Bombers?

Other Books in the At Issue Series:

At Issue

What Motivates Suicide Bombers?

Roman Espejo, Book Editor

GREENHAVEN PRESS
A part of Gale, Cengage Learning

GALE
CENGAGE Learning

Detroit • New York • San Francisco • New Haven, Conn • Waterville, Maine • London

Christine Nasso, *Publisher*
Elizabeth Des Chenes, *Managing Editor*

© 2010 Greenhaven Press, a part of Gale, Cengage Learning.

Gale and Greenhaven Press are registered trademarks used herein under license.

For more information, contact:
Greenhaven Press
27500 Drake Rd.
Farmington Hills, MI 48331-3535
Or you can visit our Internet site at gale.cengage.com

For product information and technology assistance, contact us at

Gale Customer Support, 1-800-877-4253
For permission to use material from this text or product, submit all requests online at www.cengage.com/permissions

Further permissions questions can be e-mailed to permissionrequest@cengage.com

Articles in Greenhaven Press anthologies are often edited for length to meet page requirements. In addition, original titles of these works are changed to clearly present the main thesis and to explicitly indicate the author's opinion. Every effort is made to ensure that Greenhaven Press accurately reflects the original intent of the authors. Every effort has been made to trace the owners of copyrighted material.

Cover image © Todd Davidson/Illustration Works/Corbis.

LIBRARY OF CONGRESS CATALOGING-IN-PUBLICATION DATA

What motivates suicide bombers? / Roman Espejo, book editor.
   p. cm. -- (At issue)
  Includes bibliographical references and index.
  ISBN 978-0-7377-4448-4 (hardcover)
  ISBN 978-0-7377-4449-1 (pbk.)
  1. Terrorism. 2. Suicide bombers. 3. Martyrdom--Islam. I. Espejo, Roman, 1977-
  HV6431.W43 2009
  363.325'11--dc22

                                    2009028941

Printed in the United States of America
2 3 4 5 6 7 13 12 11

Contents

Introduction

On May 17, 2009, Selvarasa Pathmanathan, head of international diplomatic relations of the Liberation Tigers of Tamil Eelam (LTTE), announced in an official statement that the organization had surrendered to the government of Sri Lanka after their quarter-century civil war. Earlier that year, the LTTE had dwindled to about 700 members, retreating to pockets of jungle in the northeast.

"We have decided to silence our guns," Pathmanathan stated. "Our only regrets are for the lives lost and that we could not hold out for longer. We can no longer bear to see the innocent blood of our people being spilled."[1] A day later, the Sri Lankan military reported that it had killed the founder and chief of the LTTE, Velupillai Prabhakaran.

The LTTE, also known as the Tamil Tigers, was established in 1976 by Prabhakaran in response to the marginalization of the Tamil ethnic group in Sri Lanka, where the majority is Sinhalese. The LTTE fought for control of the Tamil homeland, located in north and east Sri Lanka, establishing military, air, and naval forces—as well as its own court, police, and tax systems—during its rise to power. The organization achieved notoriety as fierce militants in large part because of its suicide attacks: from 1980 to 2000, the LTTE carried out 168 such missions, killing more than 500 people and injuring thousands of others. Among those missions was the May 1991 assassination of former Indian prime minister Rajiv Gandhi, in which a Tamil Tiger operative, Thenmuli Rajaratnam, detonated a vest of explosives hidden under her clothes as she greeted Gandhi. Two years later a male Tamil Tiger bomber murdered Ranasinghe Premadasa, Sri Lanka's third president, during a May Day rally. An estimated 30 percent of the organization's suicide bombers have been female, rivaling all other extremist groups. The wing responsible for these operations is called the Black Tigers.

In September 2006, four years after the LTTE and the Sri Lankan government had signed a shaky cease-fire, Menake, a female member of the Black Tigers in her mid-twenties, set out as a human bomb to the city of Colombo to assassinate Sri Lankan prime minister Ratnasiri Wickremanayake. Her instructions were to "forget the victims."[2] Three days into her mission, while surveying Wickremanayake's movements for a final time, Menake was apprehended by security guards. After taking her into custody, the guards recognized Menake as an operative because of the vial of cyanide she wore around her neck. Tamil Tigers carried such poison in case of arrest. She was sent to the Boosa Detention Center and brought back to Colombo in March 2007. Authorities hoped she could serve as an informant.

Several years earlier, in 2000, Menake's relatives, succumbing to pressure from LTTE recruiters, had handed her over to the LTTE against her will. She then completed basic training, worked in the intelligence-gathering division, and subsequently sent a letter to the Tamil Tigers' secretariat. She wrote that it "would be an honor" to join the Black Tigers. "I was depressed and in pain," Menake said of her motivations. She had been raped by her alcoholic father and treated as a burden by most of her kin. "I had nerve damage to my spine after falling from an LTTE tractor. The doctor said I might become paralyzed when I got older. I thought, *Why continue to live?* A lot of girls were volunteering to be suicide bombers, so I thought I would, too."[3] While jailed in Colombo and awaiting her future, Menake reflected, "But now, I feel I could lead a normal life. I want to live, not die." However, her offense could result in life imprisonment or a death sentence in Sri Lanka, where anti-terrorism laws are strict.

To some observers, Menake fits the profile of a suicide bomber. She had been sexually assaulted, she lacked social mobility, and she had been politically indoctrinated—her reasons for choosing a destructive path shaped by lifelong despair, radicalization, and worsening circumstances. Other suicide terrorists, however, have come from seemingly stable backgrounds. For instance, in late 2005, another female suicide bomber made headlines, and not only for her attack: She was a middle-class European whose husband was purportedly killed by American troops in Iraq. In *At Issue: What Motivates Suicide Bombers?* experts, commentators, analysts, and scholars attempt to understand the rationale behind these unthinkable acts.

Notes

1. TamilNet, May 12, 2009 http://www.tamilnet.com/art.html?catid=13&artid=29389
2. Jan Goodwin, *Marie Claire*, September 2007.
3. Jan Goodwin, *Marie Claire*, September 2007.

Islam Advocates Suicide Terrorism

World Net Daily

World Net Daily is an American conservative news website.

The U.S. government portrays Islamic extremist groups and suicide bombers as radicals who distort the Quran's teachings to justify their heinous actions. According to Pentagon briefings, intelligence analysts have concluded that these suicide terrorists are rationally acting students who study scripture dealing with jihad *(holy warfare), however. In preparation for missions, attackers—who are motivated to suicidal martyrdom by promises of honor and paradise in the afterlife—recite passages from several of the Quran's chapters and participate in religious ceremonies. Furthermore, mainstream and western Muslim religious leaders have condoned suicide bombings and praised martyrs who "kill themselves for Islam."*

With suicide bombings spreading from Iraq to Afghanistan, the Pentagon has tasked intelligence analysts to pinpoint what's driving Muslim after Muslim to do the unthinkable.

Their preliminary finding is politically explosive: it's their "holy book" the Quran after all, according to intelligence briefings obtained by WND [World Net Daily].

World Net Daily, "Suicide Bombers Follow Quran, Concludes Pentagon Briefing," *WorldNetDaily.com*, September 27, 2006. Reproduced by permission.

In public, the U.S. government has made an effort to avoid linking the terrorist threat to Islam and the Quran while dismissing suicide terrorists as crazed heretics who pervert Islamic teachings.

"The terrorists distort the idea of jihad into a call for violence and murder," the White House maintains in its recently released "National Strategy for Combating Terrorism" report.

Suicide in defense of Islam is permitted, and the Islamic suicide bomber is, in the main, a rational actor.

But internal Pentagon briefings show intelligence analysts have reached a wholly different conclusion after studying Islamic scripture and the backgrounds of suicide terrorists. They've found that most Muslim suicide bombers are in fact students of the Quran who are motivated by its violent commands—making them, as strange as it sounds to the West, "rational actors" on the Islamic stage.

In Islam, it is not how one lives one's life that guarantees spiritual salvation, but how one dies, according to the briefings. There are great advantages to becoming a martyr. Dying while fighting the infidels in the cause of Allah reserves a special place and honor in Paradise. And it earns special favor with Allah.

"Suicide in defense of Islam is permitted, and the Islamic suicide bomber is, in the main, a rational actor," concludes a recent Pentagon briefing paper titled, "Motivations of Muslim Suicide Bombers."

Suicide for Allah a 'Win-Win'

"His actions provide a win-win scenario for himself, his family, his faith and his God," the document explains. "The bomber secures salvation and the pleasures of Paradise. He earns a degree of financial security and a place for his family in Paradise. He defends his faith and takes his place in a long line of martyrs to be memorialized as a valorous fighter.

"And finally, because of the manner of his death, he is assured that he will find favor with Allah," the briefing adds. "Against these considerations, the selfless sacrifice by the individual Muslim to destroy Islam's enemies becomes a suitable, feasible and acceptable course of action."

The briefing—produced by a little-known Pentagon intelligence unit called the Counterintelligence Field Activity, or CIFA—cites a number of passages from the Quran dealing with jihad, or "holy" warfare, martyrdom and Paradise, where "beautiful mansions" and "maidens" await martyr heroes. In preparation for attacks, suicide terrorists typically recite passages from six surahs, or chapters, of the Quran: Baqura (Surah 2), Al Imran (3), Anfal (8), Tawba (9), Rahman (55) and Asr (103).

CIFA staffs hundreds of investigators and analysts to help coordinate Pentagon security efforts at U.S. military installations at home and abroad.

The Pentagon unit is especially concerned about a new wave of suicide bombings hitting Afghanistan.

Suicide bombings have killed more than 200 people in Afghanistan this year [2006], up from single digits two years ago. [In September, 2006], a suicide bomber detonated his explosive vest and killed 18 outside an Afghan government compound. [Another] suicide bomber riding a bike killed at least four NATO [North Atlantic Treaty Organization] soldiers. And earlier this month[, also in September, 2006], a suicide car bomber rammed into a U.S. military convoy near the U.S. Embassy in Kabul, killing 16 people, including two American soldiers.

500 Suicide Bombers in Reserve

The U.S. command in Afghanistan now warns that a suicide bombing cell is operating inside [Kabul,] the Afghan capital.

Meanwhile, the Taliban's top military commander told ABC News he has 500 suicide bombers at his disposal.

"We have so many of them that it is difficult to accommodate and arm and equip them," Mullah Dadullah Akhund said. "Some of them have been waiting for a year or more for their turn to be sent to the battlefield."

The emergence of a suicide cell in Kabul troubles military analysts because suicide attacks are the most effective weapon Muslim terrorists can use against the West. The [Rand Corporation] predicts they'll pose a serious and constant threat to the U.S. [United States] for years to come.

The U.S. intelligence community is growing increasingly worried, as well.

"Most jihadist groups will use suicide attacks focused primarily on soft targets [people] to implement asymmetric warfare strategy," warns the just-declassified executive summary of the National Intelligence Estimate on the global terror threat. "Fighters with experience in Iraq are a potential source of leadership for jihadists pursuing these tactics."

Many scholars and media pundits, however, insist Muslim suicide bombers are not driven by religion.

"Beneath the religious rhetoric with which [such terror] is perpetrated, it occurs largely in the service of secular aims," claims Professor Robert A. Pape of the University of Chicago. "Suicide terrorism is mainly a response to foreign occupation rather than a product of Islamic fundamentalism."

He says U.S. foreign policy is more a factor than faith.

"Though it speaks of Americans as infidels, al-Qaida is less concerned with converting us to Islam than removing us from Arab and Muslim lands," Pape said.

But what about the recent video by Adam Gadahn, the American al-Qaida [member], warning fellow Americans to convert to Islam before al-Qaida attacks again?

"He never mentions virgins or the benefits Islamic martyrs receive in Heaven," Pape asserted.

In fact, Gadahn notes 36 minutes into his speech that Allah reserves the highest rewards—"honors and delights"—for martyrs in Paradise.

Before the 9/11 attacks, the hijackers shaved and doused themselves with flower water in preparation for their weddings with the beautiful virgins in Paradise.

"[He] promised the martyr in his path the reward over and above the reward of the believer," Gadahn said. "He has promised ... honors and delights too numerous to go into here."

The 9/11 hijackers and the London bombers made martyrdom videos. In their last testaments, they recite the Quran while talking of their "love of death" and "sacrificing life for Allah." Seven martyrdom videotapes also were recovered by British authorities in the foiled transatlantic sky terror plot.

Before the 9/11 attacks, the hijackers shaved and doused themselves with flower water in preparation for their weddings with the beautiful virgins in Paradise. "Know that the women of Paradise are waiting, calling out 'Come hither, friend of Allah,'" according to a four-page letter circulated among them titled "The Last Night." "They have dressed in their most beautiful clothing."

But are the virgins scriptural or apocryphal? French documentarian Pierre Rehov, who interviewed the families of suicide bombers and would-be bombers in an attempt to find out why they do it, says it's not a myth or fantasy of heretics.

He says there's no doubt the Quran "promises virgins" to Muslim men who die while fighting infidels in jihad, and it's a key motivating factor behind suicide terrorism.

"It's obviously connected to religion," said Rehov, who features his interviews with Muslims in a recently released film, "Suicide Killers." "They really believe they are going to get the virgins."

He says would-be Muslim suicide bombers he's interviewed have shown him passages in the Quran "in which it's absolutely written that they're going to get the girls in the afterlife."

Muslim clerics do not disavow the virgins-for-martyrs reward as a perverted interpretation of the Quran.

And even Muslim leaders in the West condone suicide bombings. British scholar Azzam Tamimi recently told 8,000 Muslims in Manchester, England, that dying while fighting "[President] George [W.] Bush and [British Prime Minister] Tony Blair" is "just" and "the greatest act of martyrdom." Earlier, he said it's "the straight way to pleasing Allah."

And the founder of an allegedly mainstream Muslim group in Washington—the Council on American-Islamic Relations—also has given his blessing to suicide bombings.

Addressing a youth session at the 1999 Islamic Association for Palestine's annual convention in Chicago, CAIR [Council on American-Islamic Relations] founder Omar Ahmad praised suicide bombers who "kill themselves for Islam," according to a transcript provided by terror expert Steve Emerson's Investigative Project.

"Fighting for freedom, fighting for Islam, that is not suicide," Ahmad asserted. "They kill themselves for Islam."

Osama bin Laden has encouraged "Muslim brothers" to defeat the U.S. and U.K. [United Kingdom] with suicide attacks.

"I tell you to act upon the orders of Allah," he said in 2003, "be united against Bush and Blair and defeat them through suicide attacks so that you may be successful before Allah."

2

Islam Does Not Advocate Suicide Terrorism

Ihsanic Intelligence

Ihsanic Intelligence is an online Islamic think tank based in London, England.

The teachings of Islam do not legitimize or promote suicide bombings. This terrorism tactic does not lawfully comply with jihad, or Islamic resistance against persecution, oppression, and foreign aggression. Accordingly, a warrior who enters combat outnumbered, unarmored, or with little hope of escape and is killed by his enemies or accident is considered a martyr. The technique of suicide bombing, however, counters this definition of martyrdom as well as Islamic views against suicide and murder. In fact, the illegitimacy of suicide terrorism was not debated among Muslim scholars until recently, and those who have approved of such acts may have done so under political or social coercion.

*J*ihad, Islamic holy war, is a valid part of the Islamic tradition of legitimate martial resistance in the face of persecution, oppression and foreign aggression. As an Islamic discipline, *Jihad* can only be conducted within the parameters of the *Sunnah*, the normative practice of Prophet Muhammad, and the *Shari'ah*, the legal code he brought and which has been sustained to the present era. Suicide terrorism is an ancient tactic, which ha[s] been used by a variety of entities

Ihsanic Intelligence, "The Hijacked Caravan: Refuting Suicide Bombings as Martyrdom Operations in Contemporary *Jihad* Strategy," 2005, pp. 1–2, 7–8, 11. Copyright © MMV. Ihsanic Intelligence. All Rights Reserved. Reproduced by permission.

around the world, invoking causes such as religion, nation-hood, honour, etc. But there is disagreement amongst the scholars of Sunni Islam [the religion's largest branch] about the legitimacy of suicide bombings as a valid *Jihad* tactic in martial conflicts around the world, for they are a modern scourge [that has] emerged in the Islamic world in the last generation. On September 11th, 2001, the pan-Islamist terror-ists of the al-Qa'eda network flew commercial planes into the key military and economic buildings of the United States of America in spectacular suicide bombings. Since then, suicide bombings perpetrated by Islamist terrorists have proliferated around the globe. As the tactic has multiplied in its use and globalised, a holistic deduction based on the sources of Sunni Islam is required on the issue, providing a comprehensive refutation of the legitimacy of the act using the sources them-selves.

Refuting Claims

Claims can be made against a need to create a holistic deduc-tion regarding suicide bombing[. These claims] need to be re-futed in the first instance:

1. In the present status quo, there is a difference in opin-ion [among] Sunni scholars regarding the legitimacy of suicide bombings, and some believe that this suffices. However, prior to 1989, the issue of suicide bombing was never debated amongst Sunni scholars due to the absolute illegitimacy of the acts. The subsequent tempo-ral "success" of such operations for political aims does not automatically legitimise the [act]. Hence, the issue of suicide bombing constituting a legitimate act within Sunni Islam needs to be resolved.

2. As there is no [precedent] for a holistic deduction within Sunni Islam, it can be claimed that this is a rep-rehensible innovation and has no basis within Sunni Islam. On the contrary, holistic deductions in their es-

sence have been taken ... historically by state entities, who [have] consulted Islamic lawyers, advisers and specialists prior to ruling on a matter. This has been the case in Sunni Islam since the inception of the Caliphate [spiritual leadership] to the present-day rulers.

3. Though it can be claimed that no scholastic authority for a holistic deduction exists, it has been adduced that some eminent Sunni scholars have stated that suicide bombing is illegitimate, and therefore a case has been developed from their perspectives. Moreover, a holistic deduction can only be holistic if it has not been refuted by greater primary evidence.

4. It can be [observed] that such a holistic deduction will only serve the interests of the enemy of the Muslims, but a holistic deduction on determining the truth about a matter within Sunni Islam can only strengthen the position of Sunni Muslims to clarify their beliefs and positions on the matter.

5. Stating that suicide bombing is being used as a martial *Jihad* tactic and, therefore, cannot be discussed except by those who have performed martial *Jihad* [dismisses] the fact that not only [is] martial *Jihad* ... considered the lesser *Jihad*, in comparison to the greater *Jihad* of spiritual warfare, but that also that the vast majority of Islamic scholars today would not have participated themselves in martial *Jihad*, but are qualified to dispense legal advice on matters.

6. It can be claimed that suicide bombing in areas of immense persecution of Muslims makes the act a last resort of both defiance and desperation, but this [first] ignores the persecution as either a Divine purification or trial, [second] ignores the status of a person who is defending the land of Muslims merely by being there, and

[third] of alternative and valid techniques of *Jihad* which exist and have [been] demonstrated to be effective.

The technique of suicide bombing has become synonymous with terrorism to achieve pan-Islam, and therefore identified with the Islamic religion as a whole.

A Plethora of Evidence

There [is] a plethora of [evidence] why the need to create a holistic deduction refuting suicide bombings within Islam is required.

1. The technique of suicide bombing has become synonymous with terrorism to achieve pan-Islam, and therefore identified with the Islamic religion as a whole.

2. The number of suicide bombings committed by those invoking Islam has increased dramatically in the modern era.

3. Potential suicide bombers have *fatawwa* (pl. *fatwa*) [an interpretation of Islamic law] outlining exalted virtues of suicide bombings, when no such . . . document exists in global circulation. Some *fatawwa* are reminiscent of the Prophetic statement, "Whoever gives a fatwa without knowledge, the sin will be on the issuer." [Abu Dawud]

4. Sunni scholars who have condemned suicide bombings have never addressed the evidences from the *Shari'ah* cited by *fatawwa* for the use of potential suicide bombers.

5. Sunni scholars who condemn suicide bombing may not have voiced this opinion or given a public *fatwa*, due to opposition from other scholars and for the sake of traditional academic etiquette. However, in the interests of seeking the global optimum and public good in contemporary circumstances, a need and responsibility arises

which did not exist before. According to the Prophet, "Reliable people from each succeeding generation will carry this knowledge. They will refute the distortion of those who exaggerate and the explanations of the ignorant." [al-Baihaqi]

6. Sunni scholars who have approved the act of suicide bombing may have done so under duress from those considered oppressive and/or heretical governments though believing it to be untrue, a valid position within Sunni Islam when the threat of the religion in its orthodox form is under threat.

7. Sunni Muslims worldwide in the Islamic *Ummah* (Community) do not believe that the act of suicide bombing is sanctioned within Islam, but that it is abhorrent and a reprehensible innovation to the Prophetic Way as based on the *hadith*. Therefore, it is necessary to determine whether it truly is as the Prophet said that "every reprehensible innovation is misguidance and every misguidance is in hell" [Muslim] and that "he who inaugurates a beneficial sunnah in Islam earns the reward of it and of all who perform it after him without diminishing their own rewards in the slightest, and he who introduces a reprehensible sunnah is guilty of the sin of it and of all who perform it after him without diminishing their own sins in the slightest." [Muslim]

8. Sunni scholars who have approved the act of suicide bombing may have done so with the correct intention, but arrived at an erroneous legal deduction in which case the optimum holistic deduction is sought, which should be comprehensive, transparent and suitable for global dissemination. This need is based on the Prophet's statement that "If a judge has exercised his judgment, and been proven correct, then he has two rewards. And if he judged and was mistaken, then he has one reward." [Muslim]

9. Sunni Muslims have been given numerous and substantiated *fatawwa* on the legitimacy of suicide bombings, making it necessary to determine whether the Prophet would have approved such an act. He said, when asked about righteousness: "Consult your heart. Righteousness is that about which the soul feels tranquil and the heart feels tranquil, and wrongdoing is that which wavers in the soul and moves to and fro in the chest, even though people have repeatedly given you *fatawwa* [on the subject]." [Ibn Hanbal and al-Darimi]

10. As the tactic is becoming synonymous with Islam, consensus is also required on the issue, as the Prophet said, "My *Ummah* shall not agree on error." [al-Hakim]. . . .

The Specifity of Suicide Bombings

In the *fatwa*, suicide bombings are included under a broad definition of different techniques [of] martyrdom operations. However, within these different techniques, only suicide bombing can be deemed unlawful. The technique of one-man armies plunging into the enemy without armour or little chance of escape as a martyrdom operation is valid, precisely because the warrior is killed by his enemy, and does not kill himself. In addition, the one who accidentally kills himself with a weapon he is brandishing is also considered a martyr, as he never had the intention to kill himself. However, suicide bombing necessitates that the suicide bomber in a premeditated fashion blows himself up with his own hand in an act which is not only *haram* [unlawful] but a reprehensible innovatory martyrdom operation [RIMO], as it is antithetical and anathema [despicable] to a genuine martyrdom operation. The person committing [it] kills himself in [an] act which they believe to [be] Islamic when it is actually a reprehensible innovation in contemporary *Jihad* strategy. The term can be translated in Arabic as *"al-amliyat al-istishadiya al-*

bidiyyah al-dalalliyah" or *"al-amliyat al-intihariyyah".* It is a historical fact that there has never been a recorded instance of suicide terrorism within the history of Sunni Islam, though it has occurred historically in all other major civilisations and religions. Moreover, apart from being reprehensible innovations, suicide bombings are the equivalent to the enormity of the sin of murder, the most heinous sin in Islam only after associating partners with Allah.

Allah's advice to His creation is very clear and explicitly prohibits a person taking his or her own life, whether in civilian life or on a Jihad mission.

Suicide Bombing as Suicide and Murder

There are a plethora of *hadith* [oral traditions] which determine that the technique of suicide bombings can be deemed suicidal and murderous acts within Islam and are forbidden according to these evidences:

I. Suicide

1. ETERNAL DAMNATION OF SUICIDE

"Do not kill yourselves. Verily, Allah is Merciful to you. And, whoever does that, out of aggression and injustice. We shall burn him in a Fire. And that is easy for Allah." [Holy Qur'an, 4:29–30]

Allah's advice to His creation is very clear and explicitly prohibits a person taking his or her own life, whether in civilian life or on a *Jihad* mission. The scholars of Sunni Islam have accepted the protection of life as the primary aim of the *Shari'ah*, within the maxim, 'Every *Shari'ah* came to protect five values: life, intellect, faith, lineage and property.'

2. ONE'S OWN [HAND] IN SELF-DESTRUCTION

"And spend of your substance in the cause of Allah, and make not your own hands contribute to [your] destruction; but do good; for Allah loves those who do good." [Holy Qur'an, 2:195]

This verse acquires relevant significance with regards to the illegitimacy of the suicide bombings, as Allah is warning [men] not to make their "own hands" contribute to their destruction, as the vast majority of suicide bombings in history are committed by the perpetrators detonating the charges in their hands. The Prophet has commented on this verse as mentioned above.

3. THE MEANS OF SUICIDE IN THE HEREAFTER

The Prophet said, "He who killed himself with a thing would be tormented on the Day of Resurrection with that very thing. It is not for a man to offer that which he does not own." [Muslim]

"Whoever strangles himself will be strangling himself in the Fire, and whoever stabs himself will be stabbing himself in the Fire." [al-Bukhari and Muslim] The Prophet said, *"He who commits suicide by stabbing himself with an iron [blade] shall ... have that iron [blade] in his hand, and he will thrust it into his body in the fire of Hell, remaining therein forever [in that state], and whoever took poison and killed himself, then he will drink it in the Fire of Hell, remaining therein forever [in that state], and whoever threw himself off a mountain and killed himself, then he will be falling in the Fire of Hell, remaining therein for ever [in that state]."* [al-Bukhari and Muslim]

4. SUICIDE IN *JIHAD*

"Among those before you, there was a man with a wound, and he was in anguish, so he took a knife and cut his hands, and the blood did not stop until he died. Allah said, "My servant has hastened the ending of his life, so I prohibit Paradise to him." [al-Bukhari and Muslim]

This *hadith* demonstrates that the *mujahid* [person who partakes in *jihad*] who takes his own life, due to his own anguish,

23

commits the act of hastening the end of his life, which he has no right to do. Allah owns the man's life and no man can know the precise moment of his death, unless he hastens it by . . . cutting himself due to a lack of patience and despair. The consequence is eternal damnation. . . .

Murder is a heinous crime in Islam, with devastating consequences in the next world, and the suicide bomber murders when he detonates himself, as civilian bystanders are always killed.

II. Murder

1. KILLING OF ONE PERSON

"So, We decreed for the tribe of Israel that if someone kills another person—unless it is in retaliation for someone else or for causing corruption in the earth—it is as if he had murdered all of mankind." [Holy Qur'an, 5:32]

Murder is a heinous crime in Islam, with devastating consequences in the next world, and the suicide bomber murders when he detonates himself, as civilian bystanders are always killed.

2. KILLING OF MUSLIMS

"As for anyone who kills a mu'min [believing Muslim] deliberately, his repayment is Hell, remaining in it timelessly, forever. Allah is angry with him and has cursed him, and has prepared from a terrible punishment." [Holy Qur'an, 4:92]

Any suicide bomber who kills Muslims deliberately faces eternal damnation. In this regard, the Prophet also said, *"The cessation of the temporal world is less significant to Allah than the killing of a single Muslim person."* [al-Nasai]

3. KILLING OF NON-MUSLIMS

The Prophet said, "*Whoever killed a person having a treaty with the Muslims shall not smell the fragrance of Paradise though its fragrance is perceived from a distance of forty years*" [al-Bukhari].

The Prophet also said in this regard, "*Beware! Whoever is cruel and hard on [members of] a non-Muslim minority, or curtails their rights, or burdens them in more than they can bear, or takes anything from them against their free will; I will complain against the person on the Day of Judgment*" [al-Bukhari]. If a government in a Muslim land has gained a treaty with a protected minority, ensuring their safety and security, then their life and wealth are protected, it is not permissible to harm him, and whoever kills him, then "*he will not smell the smell of Paradise.*" Sanctuary and refuge is to be given to the non-Muslim citizen who requests it: *When Umm Hani granted sanctuary to a man from the polytheists in the Year of the Conquest, and when Ali ibn Abi Talib desired to kill him, she went to the Prophet, and informed him [of that] so he said: "We have granted sanctuary to the one you have granted sanctuary, O Umm Hani."* [al-Bukhari and Muslim] Therefore the one who has entered a Muslim-majority land in the present day, and has the ... agreement of personal security, then it is not permissible to violate his rights within the *Shari'ah*.

4. KILLING OF WOMEN AND CHILDREN

The Prophet forbade the killing of women and children. [Malik]

The Prophet forbade killing women and children in *Jihad*, whereas the suicide bomber's murder victims can include women and children. It is narrated on the authority of Ibn Umar that a woman was found killed in one of the battles; so the Messenger of Allah forbade the killing of women and children. Though it has been reported that there were instances of "collateral damage" during night-raids by Muslim commanders, where women and children may have been unknown [victims], Ibn Abbas, the prime interpreter of the Holy Qur'an, said, *"The Messenger of Allah did not kill the children of the enemy, so you should not kill the children."* [Muslim] Therefore, we can determine that the explicit injunction of Islam is that women, children, the sick and the religious devotees are not be to be killed. Regarding the deployment of females during war, their professions were always ancillary and in support services, like nursing and water-carriers: *"The Messenger of Allah allowed Umm Sulaym and some other women of the Ansar to accompany him when he went to war; they would give water to the soldiers and would treat the wounded."* [Muslim] Utilising women and children in operations or targeting them or considering the[m] collateral [damage] is forbidden by the *Shari'ah. . . .*

3

Al Qaeda Uses Mass Media to Encourage Global Suicide Terrorism

Yoram Schweitzer and Sari Goldstein Ferber

Yoram Schweitzer is senior research fellow and director of the Program on Terrorism and Low Intensity Conflict at the Institute for National Security Studies (INSS) in Tel Aviv, Israel. Sari Goldstein Ferber is director of developmental care at the Sackler School of Medicine at Tel Aviv University.

Al Qaeda, the Islamic extremist group responsible for the September 11 attacks, promotes suicide terrorism worldwide to create fear within the Western world and influence public opinion and policy. Using the mass media, Al Qaeda advances its propaganda through the release of professionally produced videos and interviews with sympathetic journalists. The group also uses the Internet to recruit new suicide volunteers, providing instructions on how to make explosives and carry out bombings as well as a list of targets. Moreover, Al Qaeda capitalizes on the publicity created by its own attacks—and those linked to its affiliates—to strengthen its message of a global jihad, or holy war.

Al-Qaeda has emerged over the years as an organization with a flexible and dynamic structure engaged in global activity. It has undergone changes in membership, leadership, and command locations since its establishment. The ideal of

Yoram Schweitzer and Sari Goldstein Ferber, *Al Qaeda and the Internationalization of Suicide Terrorism*, Tel Aviv, Israel: The Jaffee Center for Strategic Studies (JCSS), 2005, pp. 27–32. Copyright © 2005 Jaffee Center for Strategic Studies. All rights reserved. Reproduced by permission.

al-Qaeda's globalization is actualized through the dispersal of al-Qaeda training [camp] "alumni" in locations around the world; the organization's aspiration to provide a model for emulation by other, and not necessarily local, groups; its extensive propaganda campaign; and the use of modern communications media and the Internet.

The Dispersal of the Afghan Alumni

Al-Qaeda's main objective was to promote self-sacrifice among as many Islamic organizations as possible, primarily those identifying with the concept of global jihad. In addition, the organization's glorification of suicide attacks appears to have been of special sectoral symbolic importance. The phenomenon of Muslim suicide terrorism in the name of Allah was generally associated with the Shiite stream of Islam, which was responsible for the introduction of this mode of operation during the 1980s. Thus, from the perspective of al-Qaeda leaders, the organization's entrance into the arena of suicide terrorist operators had to dwarf the suicide attacks that had already been carried out by other groups both in scope and in damage, in order to increase the global prestige of Sunni Islam and the prestige of al-Qaeda and its leader.

[Founder Osama] Bin Laden has worked to send clear signals that suicide terrorism is a weapon of defiance challenging the Western way of life.

A Model for Emulation

Al-Qaeda worked towards achieving mass death [in proportions] as high ... as possible. To this end, the group and its affiliates used especially large groups of suicide terrorists, numbering in certain circumstances twelve, fourteen, nineteen, or, in the case of Chechnya, thirty. These attacks indeed resulted in an unprecedented number of casualties. The number of terrorists was . . . unusual in comparison to most other terrorist organizations that had carried out suicide operations, with the exception of the Tamil Tigers . . . in Sri Lanka, [who] at times [used] cells with a larger number of members, with as many as a dozen participants in one operation.

The Propaganda Campaign

Al-Qaeda cast the suicide weapon as an effective tool for deterring the West—first and foremost the United States—from aggression, and for instilling fear in targeted populations around the globe. [Founder Osama] Bin Laden has worked to send clear signals that suicide terrorism is a weapon of defiance challenging the Western way of life. Mass indiscriminate killing is designed to plant a strong sense of fear and vulnerability, which in turn would spur public opinion in Western countries to pressure their governments to adjust their policies and yield to [Bin Laden's] various demands. Bin Laden also uses propaganda and psychological warfare techniques that exacerbate the physical harm inflicted. Al-Qaeda and its affiliates tend to issue press releases or videotapes shortly after attacks, reiterating each attack's background and threatening to repeat and intensify attacks if the countries targeted do not change their policies. Group leaders may even address public opinion directly in order to encourage civilians to exert pressure on their governments.

For example, following the October 2002 attacks in Bali by al-Jama'a al-Islamiya with the assistance of al-Qaeda, which claimed the lives of 202 victims, Bin Laden released a cassette in which he threatened to attack Australia a second time, claiming that Australia was cooperating with the United States and harming Muslims through its policy in East Timor. In a similar manner, shortly after attacks in Madrid killed 191 people on March 11, 2004, Bin Laden issued a manifest accusing the Spanish government of responsibility for the attack, due to its support for the United States and the presence of its troops in Iraq. Exploiting the trauma of the attacks, he called for the citizens of Europe to pressure their governments to withdraw their forces from Iraq, in exchange for which they would receive a *hudna* (a temporary ceasefire). This generous offer, he threatened, would be rescinded in three months, after which the attacks in Europe would be renewed.

The Electronic Media and the Internet

Al-Qaeda uses modern communications media . . . for the dissemination of the core organizational concepts, chief among them self-sacrifice in the path of Allah, and for strategic direction towards preferred targets of operation for supporters of global jihad. Indeed, Arab and Western mass media have been primary tools of al-Qaeda commanders in increasing the organization's strength in areas not under their direct control. A further objective has been increasing the prestige of the Arab media, which has always been considered inferior and of little interest compared to its Western counterparts.

Recognizing the potential of the media, al-Qaeda established a communications committee, which was headed for a long period by Khaled Sheikh Muhammad, before he became one of the organization's top operational commanders. At the same time, Bin Laden created a company called al-Sahab, which produced the professional tapes and promotional film clips disseminated throughout the Arab and Western world, primarily by means of the Qatari television station al-Jazeera. The preferred status that Bin Laden granted al-Jazeera and [select] sympathetic journalists such as Yosri Fouda (the journalist given the first exclusive with Khaled Sheikh Muhammad and his close colleague Ramzi Bin al-Shibh just before the first anniversary of the September 11 attacks) and Ahmed Zeidan (the al-Jazeera correspondent in Pakistan who was allowed to interview Bin Laden in Afghanistan a number of times before the American invasion of the country) was part of Bin Laden's calculated media policy. Bin Laden even admitted to Zeidan that al-Qaeda selects sympathetic journalists and initiates granting them interviews.

The media played a pivotal role in al-Qaeda's claim of responsibility for the September 11 attacks. Until September 11, Bin Laden had refrained from explicit claims of responsibility for attacks carried out by al-Qaeda, both from his desire to remain unexposed to reprisal attacks, and, more importantly, to prevent the leader of the Taliban from issuing an explicit order to refrain from causing trouble for the regime. The regime was already under international pressure due to its role in the drug trade and terrorism, and was told to turn Bin Laden over to the United States and to close the terrorist training camps within its borders. At first, then, Bin Laden did not claim direct responsibility for September 11 either. Despite the fact that his hints and innuendos on the subject were clear to everyone listening, they left him room to maneuver and to enjoy the fruits of his achievement without actually providing legal proof of his guilt. Yet after the American attack on Afghanistan and the American-led international coalition's declaration of war, a process began, in December 2001, through which Bin Laden indirectly admitted that he had been responsible for the attack. Eventually, al-Qaeda took responsibility for the attacks in the United States in an unequivocal public declaration, in the form of a three-part series of hour-long segments of an al-Jazeera program called *It Was Top Secret*, directed by al-Jazeera correspondent Yosri Fouda. This series was initiated by al-Qaeda, and its broadcast of the segments was timed to coincide with the first anniversary of the September 11 attacks.

Critical here is al-Qaeda's understanding of the role of the media, clearly reflected in a letter from Ramzi Bin al-Shibh, assistant to the commander of the US attacks, to Yosri Fouda, the correspondent chosen for the organization's announcement of responsibility:

It is the obligation of he who works in a field capable of influencing public opinion to be faithful to Allah in his work ... not satisfying human beings ... and not aspir[ing] to material benefit or fame. [You should] put the events of 9/11 and what subsequently occurred in this Crusade against Muslims in the historical and religious context of the conflict between Muslims and Christians ... so that the picture is complete in the mind of the viewers. This is a historical responsibility in the first place; for, unlike what has been promoted in the media, the ongoing war is not between America and the al-Qaeda organisation.

The close attention to media appearance is reflected in a fax from al-Qaeda to Fouda, which explained how, in the view of the sender, the three-part program should be organized and who should be interviewed, and noted the prohibition of any musical accompaniment for quotes from the Quran and the Hadith [oral traditions]. The fax said that Fouda would be expected to prepare the segments with an understanding of his mission as a Muslim journalist for Islam.

The Internet has provided young Muslims, particularly in Europe, with a virtual community that serves primarily to ease the emotional strain on Muslim immigrants experiencing the difficulties of adapting to a new environment and feeling a need to maintain their religious identity.

Furthermore, Bin Laden's clear awareness of media particulars, including the quality and angles of filming, was demonstrated when he asked Ahmed Zeidan to film him from a different angle and to disregard previous footage that, in his opinion, was not flattering. Bin Laden also directed Zeidan to refilm a ballad that he played before an audience of listeners because there was too small an audience in the original footage. Zeidan made explicit notes of his impression of Bin Laden as someone who distinguishes clearly between body language and spoken language, and keenly takes both into consideration. Bin Laden stressed to Zeidan his view of the role of the media, and, most importantly, the role of satellite television stations "that the public and the people really like, that transmit body language before spoken language. This is often the most important thing for activating the Arab street and creating pressure on governments to limit their reliance on the United States."

Al-Qaeda's communications warfare has spanned satellite television stations and the Internet. Television stations throughout the Arab world, and primarily the popular al-Jazeera network, have served al-Qaeda by broadcasting the videos produced by the organization. Bin Laden also tried to use Zeidan to refute the words of Abdallah Azam's son-in-law in the newspaper *al-Sharq al-Awsat*, which could be construed to indicate conflicts between Bin Laden and Azam, and hinted that Bin Laden was behind the assassination of his spiritual guide. During the past few years as well, while Bin Laden and Zawahiri have been the target[s] of intensive pursuit, the two still make sure to appear from time to time in audio and video tapes that they have produced meticulously, in order to prove that they are still alive and active.

In addition, the past years have witnessed increased use of the Internet by al-Qaeda and its affiliates. Out of the approximately 4,000 Islamic websites on the Internet, about 300 are connected to radical Islamic groups that support al-Qaeda. These websites disseminate the organization's messages and encourage the recruitment of new suicide volunteers to join the ranks of the global jihad. Some even provide their readers with instructions for carrying out attacks and making explosive devices, and all terrorist groups maintain more than one website in more than one language. Two Internet newsletters directly associated with al-Qaeda are *Saut al-Jihad* and *Mu'askar al-Batar*. These two websites provide explanations on how to kidnap, poison, and murder people, as well as a list of targets that should be attacked. Due to efforts by Western forces to close or damage terrorist sites, they regularly change their Internet addresses. Sometimes new addresses appear as messages for previous users, and in some cases addresses are maintained for chat rooms only, where they are passed on by chat participants.

Both the terrorists who executed the Madrid attacks in March 2004 and those who participated in the September 11 attacks made regular use of the Internet for communication. The anonymity of the web facilitates communication on sensitive issues without exposure, and thus to a certain degree neutralizes pressure from governments. The Internet has provided young Muslims, particularly in Europe, with a virtual community that serves primarily to ease the emotional strain on Muslim immigrants experiencing the difficulties of adapting to a new environment and feeling a need to maintain their religious identity. The psychological support enables them to mitigate the alienation felt by many Muslims in a foreign religious environment and to dull the sense of crisis that accompanies most instances of immigration. Indeed, the Internet actualizes the value of the Islamic *umma* [community] by making it an accessible ideal and enabling Muslims to create transnational, cross-border communities.

Through cyberspace, Internet users can receive instructions regarding religious activities in the form of verses from the Quran or oral law and can receive militant messages to quash personal misgivings regarding violent activity. Sometimes, those responsible for maintaining al-Qaeda websites are involved with al-Qaeda operational activity, as in the case of the al-Qaeda website editor apprehended in Saudi Arabia at the site where authorities recovered the body of Paul Johnson, a Lockheed Martin employee who was kidnapped and then killed by his abductors on January 18, 2004.

Thus, al-Qaeda has made sure to utilize all channels of the media to capitalize fully on its own terrorist attacks, and more significantly, the attacks carried out by its affiliates. In doing this, the organization has attributed operational successes to the organization and to the idea of global jihad, and has strengthened the power of the message of *istishhad* [martyrdom].

4

Some Islamic Schools Groom Suicide Bombers

Atia Abawi

Atia Abawi is a correspondent for CNN.

Schools operated by Islamic extremists groom youths to become suicide bombers. The Taliban and other armed groups enlist teenagers through coercion and trickery, and even under the pretext of offering a legitimate education. At these schools, recruiters indoctrinate students with fanatical interpretations of the Quran, instructing them that it is their religious duty to kill American soldiers and their allies, who allegedly murder Muslims. After completing their studies, the young men are sent on suicide missions; those caught are convicted of terrorism and placed in juvenile detention.

Kabul, Afghanistan (CNN)—A 14-year-old who was trained to kill by radicals in the tribal regions of Pakistan now sits in a crowded classroom at a detention facility in Kabul. His only wish is to see his parents again.

"I miss my parents, my mom and dad," Shakirullah says in soft tones. Like others in tribal regions, he goes by one name.

Shakirullah is already a convicted terrorist for planning to carry out a suicide bombing. He says Muslim radicals lied and tricked him into becoming a would-be bomber. "I have been detained for trying to commit a suicide attack," he says.

He says his recruiters told him it was his mission as a Muslim to kill British and American soldiers because they were killing Muslims.

Atia Abawi, "Teen Trained to Be Suicide Bomber Feels Tricked," *CNN.com*, January 2, 2009. Reproduced by permission.

They told him that once he blew himself up he wouldn't die because God would save him for being a true Muslim.

Asked what he now thinks of Americans and Westerners, Shakirullah is calm, but quick in his response.

"I don't know. God knows what type of people they are, whether they are good or bad. I don't know them," he says.

Shakirullah now passes his hours in a cell block at a juvenile detention facility in Kabul. He is serving at least five years in detention. He is to be transferred to an adult prison in a couple of years, authorities say.

He hasn't heard from his family in the Northwest Frontier Province of Pakistan. He tried to send them a letter through the International Committee of the Red Cross but is not sure it reached them.

"I don't know what they are thinking. They have no news of me," he says.

With the increased violence in Afghanistan ... more and more children [are] being recruited by armed groups and national forces.

On this day, Shakirullah attends a rehabilitation class, easily lost in the crowd of boys with shaved heads. All of the children are convicted for various crimes, including theft, fighting and even murder.

Three boys like Shakirullah are here, all guilty of planning to kill themselves and others after being recruited by terrorist groups.

With the increased violence in Afghanistan, international observers say they have seen more and more children being recruited by armed groups and national forces. The Taliban, which ruled Afghanistan with its strict Islamic rule from 1996 to 2001, has regrouped and launched a fierce insurgency.

"As you see in many places in the world, children are being used in armed conflict. They've been recruited as child soldiers; they've been recruited as armed groups. And the phenomena is now impacting, again, Afghanistan," says Catherine Mbengue, the UNICEF representative in Afghanistan.

Inside the detention center, Shakirullah walks up to his cell, his sandals sliding across the tile floor.

The cell block is empty and has metal bunk beds lined across the wall and a television set, ready for the times they have electricity. Shakirullah shares this space with 10 other boys. He sits in the center of the room with a blanket draped around him.

He barely makes eye contact and looks away as soon as he does. He is shy, but forthright in his words. "I didn't want to do it but he forced me to go," he says of his recruiter.

Rubbing his face with his hand, he says he now spends his time dreaming of his life back home in rural Pakistan. His eyes begin to water and his voice becomes softer when he talks about missing his mother.

Asked what he misses most about her, he says simply, "A mother is a mother."

His was a life of farming and tranquility in Pakistan, he says. It was also a life that took a drastic turn when his father decided to send Shakirullah for studies at a madrassa.

He says his dad wanted him to learn more about Islam and the Quran, something he could not do himself. He says his father didn't know radicals ran the school.

In the madrassa, Shakirullah learned to recite the Quran in Arabic, not his native language. He relied solely on the fanatical interpretations the mullahs were giving him.

"When I finished reciting the Quran, a mullah then came to me and told me, 'Now that you have finished the Quran, you need to go and commit a suicide attack.' That I should go to Afghanistan to commit a suicide attack," he says.

The teenager wasn't given the chance to say goodbye to his parents or siblings when he was driven to the Pakistan-Afghan border and handed over to strangers.

He says he was taken to the southeastern province of Khost, a hotbed for terrorist activity in Afghanistan. Suicide attacks have risen in Afghanistan since the U.S.-led invasion to topple the Taliban began in late 2001, after the 9/11 attacks on New York and the Pentagon.

"When I finished reciting the Quran, a mullah then came to me and told me, 'Now that you have finished the Quran, you need to go and commit a suicide attack.' That I should go to Afghanistan to commit a suicide attack," he says.

Shakirullah says that before the police arrested him, he was learning how to drive a car but that he was not sure how he was supposed to carry out his attack.

Khost is the province where a suicide car bomb went off near a voter registration site this past Sunday, killing 16 people, 14 of whom were children.

At the juvenile detention facility, Shakirullah and the others are now being taught a different interpretation of Islam.

"The teachers educate them on Islam, and explain to them that the acts that they were doing is not right for them and for others," says Mir Fayaz ah-Din, who works and lives with the boys at the facility, mentoring them and helping them in their rehabilitation.

"The way you want to kill yourself and someone else—it in itself is a big offense in Islam."

Shakirullah now says of his recruiters, "They cheated me."

5

Foreign Occupation Motivates Suicide Bombers

Robert Pape

Robert Pape is a political science professor at the University of Chicago and author of Dying to Win: The Logic of Suicide Terrorism.

A wealth of information reveals that suicide attacks are not motivated by religious, particularly Islamic, fundamentalism, but by foreign occupation. The main objective of every major suicide campaign across the world is to compel a state or government to withdraw its military forces from the terrorist group's homeland. In fact, suicide terrorism as it is known today began with secular practitioners, the Sri Lankan separatist organization Tamil Tigers, which devised the suicide vest that has been copied by Palestinian bombers. While still requiring foreign occupation, religion becomes a factor in suicide terrorism only if religious differences exist between the occupier and the occupied.

> *Last month [June 2005], Scott McConnell caught up with Associate Professor Robert Pape of the University of Chicago, whose book on suicide terrorism,* Dying to Win, *is beginning to receive wide notice. Pape has found that the most common American perceptions about who the terrorists are and what motivates them are off by a wide margin. In his office is the world's largest database of information about suicide terrorists, rows and rows of manila folders containing articles and biographical snippets in dozens of languages, compiled by Pape and teams of graduate students, a trove of data that has*

been sorted and analyzed and which underscores the great need for reappraising the [George W.] Bush administration's current strategy. Below are excerpts from a conversation with the man who knows more about suicide terrorists than any other American.

*T*he American Conservative: *Your new book,* Dying to Win, *has a subtitle:* The Logic of Suicide Terrorism. *Can you just tell us generally on what the book is based, what kind of research went into it, and what your findings were?*

Robert Pape: [From 2003 to 2005] I . . . collected the first complete database of every suicide-terrorist attack around the world from 1980 to early 2004. This research is conducted not only in English but also in native-language sources—Arabic, Hebrew, Russian, and Tamil, and others—so that we can gather information not only from newspapers, but also from products from the terrorist community. The terrorists are often quite proud of what they do in their local communities, and they produce albums and all kinds of other information that can be very helpful to understand suicide-terrorist attacks.

This wealth of information creates a new picture about what is motivating suicide terrorism. Islamic fundamentalism is not as closely associated with suicide terrorism as many people think. The world leader in suicide terrorism is a group that you may not be familiar with: the Tamil Tigers in Sri Lanka.

This is a Marxist group, a completely secular group that draws from the Hindu families of the Tamil regions of the country. They invented the famous suicide vest for their suicide assassination of [former prime minister of India] Rajiv Gandhi in May 1991. The Palestinians got the idea of the suicide vest from the Tamil Tigers.

So if Islamic fundamentalism is not necessarily a key variable behind these groups, what is?

The central fact is that overwhelmingly suicide-terrorist attacks are not driven by religion as much as they are by a clear strategic objective: to compel modern democracies to withdraw military forces from the territory that the terrorists view as their homeland. From Lebanon to Sri Lanka to Chechnya to Kashmir to the West Bank, every major suicide-terrorist campaign—over 95 percent of all the incidents—has had as its central objective to compel a democratic state to withdraw.

That would seem to run contrary to a view that one heard during the American election campaign, put forth by people who favor Bush's policy. That is, we need to fight the terrorists over there, so we don't have to fight them here.

Since suicide terrorism is mainly a response to foreign occupation and not Islamic fundamentalism, the use of heavy military force to transform Muslim societies over there, if you would, is only likely to increase the number of suicide terrorists coming at us.

Osama bin Laden's speeches and sermons . . . [b]egin by calling tremendous attention to the presence of tens of thousands of American combat forces on the Arabian Peninsula.

Since 1990, the United States has stationed tens of thousands of ground troops on the Arabian Peninsula, and that is the main mobilization appeal of Osama bin Laden and al-Qaeda. People who make the argument that it is a good thing to have them attacking us over there are missing that suicide terrorism is not a supply-limited phenomenon where there are just a few hundred around the world willing to do it because they are religious fanatics. It is a demand-driven phenomenon. That is, it is driven by the presence of foreign forces on the territory that the terrorists view as their homeland. The operation in Iraq has stimulated suicide terrorism and has given suicide terrorism a new lease on life.

If we were to back up a little bit before the invasion of Iraq to what happened before 9/11, what was the nature of the agit-

prop [propaganda meant to agitate] that Osama bin Laden and al-Qaeda were putting out to attract people?

Osama bin Laden's speeches and sermons run 40 and 50 pages long. They begin by calling tremendous attention to the presence of tens of thousands of American combat forces on the Arabian Peninsula.

In 1996, he went on to say that there was a grand plan by the United States—that the Americans were going to use combat forces to conquer Iraq, break it into three pieces, give a piece of it to Israel so that Israel could enlarge its country, and then do the same thing to Saudi Arabia. As you can see, we are fulfilling his prediction, which is of tremendous help in his mobilization appeals.

The fact that we had troops stationed on the Arabian Peninsula was not a very live issue in American debate at all. How many Saudis and other people in the Gulf were conscious of it?

We would like to think that if we could keep a low profile with our troops that it would be okay to station them in foreign countries. The truth is, we did keep a fairly low profile. We did try to keep them away from Saudi society in general, but the key issue with American troops is their actual combat power. Tens of thousands of American combat troops, married with air power, is a tremendously powerful tool.

Now, of course, today we have 150,000 troops on the Arabian Peninsula, and we are more in control of the Arabian Peninsula than ever before.

If you were to break down causal factors, how much weight would you put on a cultural rejection of the West and how much weight on the presence of American troops on Muslim territory?

The evidence shows that the presence of American troops is clearly the pivotal factor driving suicide terrorism.

If Islamic fundamentalism were the pivotal factor, then we should see some of the largest Islamic fundamentalist countries in the world, like Iran, which has 70 million people—three times the population of Iraq and three times the population of Saudi Arabia—with some of the most active groups in suicide terrorism against the United States. However, there has never been an al-Qaeda suicide terrorist from Iran, and we have no evidence that there are any suicide terrorists in Iraq from Iran.

Before our invasion, Iraq never had a suicide terrorist attack in its history.

Sudan is a country of 21 million people. Its government is extremely Islamic fundamentalist. The ideology of Sudan was so congenial to Osama bin Laden that he spent three years in Sudan in the 1990s. Yet there has never been an al-Qaeda suicide terrorist from Sudan.

I have the first complete set of data on every al-Qaeda suicide terrorist from 1995 to early 2004, and they are not from some of the largest Islamic fundamentalist countries in the world. Two thirds are from the countries where the United States has stationed heavy combat troops since 1990.

Another point in this regard is Iraq itself. Before our invasion, Iraq never had a suicide-terrorist attack in its history. Never. Since our invasion, suicide terrorism has been escalating rapidly with 20 attacks in 2003, 48 in 2004, and over 50 in just the first five months of 2005. Every year that the United States has stationed 150,000 combat troops in Iraq, suicide terrorism has doubled.

So your assessment is that there are more suicide terrorists or potential suicide terrorists today than there were in March 2003?

I have collected demographic data from around the world on the 462 suicide terrorists since 1980 who completed the mission, actually killed themselves. This information tells us that most are walk-in volunteers. Very few are criminals. Few are actually longtime members of a terrorist group. For most suicide terrorists, their first experience with violence is their very own suicide-terrorist attack.

There is no evidence there were any suicide-terrorist organizations lying in wait in Iraq before our invasion. What is
happening is that the suicide terrorists have been produced by
the invasion.

Do we know who is committing suicide terrorism in Iraq?
Are they primarily Iraqis or walk-ins from other countries in the
region?

Our best information at the moment is that the Iraqi suicide terrorists are coming from two groups—Iraqi Sunnis and
Saudis—the two populations most vulnerable to transforma-
tion by the presence of large American combat troops on the
Arabian Peninsula. This is perfectly consistent with the strategic logic of suicide terrorism.

Does al-Qaeda have the capacity to launch attacks on the
United States, or are they too tied down in Iraq? Or have they
made a strategic decision not to attack the United States, and if
so, why?

Al-Qaeda appears to have made a deliberate decision not
to attack the United States in the short term. We know this
not only from the pattern of their attacks but because we have
an actual al-Qaeda planning document found by Norwegian
intelligence. The document says that al-Qaeda should not try
to attack the continent of the United States in the short term
but instead should focus its energies on hitting America's allies in order to try to split the coalition.

What the document then goes on to do is analyze whether
they should hit Britain, Poland, or Spain. It concludes that
they should hit Spain just before the March 2004 elections because, and I am quoting almost verbatim: Spain could not
withstand two, maximum three, blows before withdrawing
from the coalition, and then others would fall like dominoes.

That is exactly what happened. Six months after the document was produced, al-Qaeda attacked Spain in Madrid. That
caused Spain to withdraw from the coalition. Others have followed. So al-Qaeda certainly has demonstrated the capacity to

attack and in fact they have done over 15 suicide-terrorist attacks since 2002, more than all the years before 9/11 combined. Al-Qaeda is not weaker now. Al-Qaeda is stronger.

What would constitute a victory in the War on Terror or at least an improvement in the American situation?

For us, victory means not sacrificing any of our vital interests while also not having Americans vulnerable to suicide-terrorist attacks. In the case of the Persian Gulf, that means we should pursue a strategy that secures our interest in oil but does not encourage the rise of a new generation of suicide terrorists.

In the 1970s and the 1980s, the United States secured its interest in oil without stationing a single combat soldier on the Arabian Peninsula. Instead, we formed an alliance with Iraq and Saudi Arabia, which we can now do again. We relied on numerous aircraft carriers off the coast of the Arabian Peninsula, and naval air power now is more effective not less. We also built numerous military bases so that we could move large numbers of ground forces to the region quickly if a crisis emerged.

That strategy, called "offshore balancing," worked splendidly against Saddam Hussein in 1990 and is again our best strategy to secure our interest in oil while preventing the rise of more suicide terrorists.

Osama bin Laden and other al-Qaeda leaders also talked about the "Crusaders-Zionist alliance," and I wonder if that, even if we weren't in Iraq, would not foster suicide terrorism. Even if the policy had helped bring about a Palestinian state, I don't think that would appease the more hardcore opponents of Israel.

I not only study the patterns of where suicide terrorism has occurred but also where it hasn't occurred. Not every foreign occupation has produced suicide terrorism. Why do some and not others? Here is where religion matters, but not quite in the way most people think. In virtually every instance where an occupation has produced a suicide-terrorist campaign, there has been a religious difference between the occupier and the occupied community. That is true not only in places such as Lebanon and in Iraq today but also in Sri Lanka, where it is the Sinhala Buddhists who are having a dispute with the Hindu Tamils.

When there is a religious difference between the occupier and the occupied, that enables terrorist leaders to demonize the occupier in especially vicious ways. Now, that still requires the occupier to be there. Absent the presence of foreign troops, Osama bin Laden could make his arguments but there wouldn't be much reality behind them. The reason that it is so difficult for us to dispute those arguments is because we really do have tens of thousands of combat soldiers sitting on the Arabian Peninsula.

Has the next generation of anti-American suicide terrorists already been created? Is it too late to wind this down, even assuming your analysis is correct and we could de-occupy Iraq?

Many people worry that once a large number of suicide terrorists have acted that it is impossible to wind it down. The history of the last 20 years, however, shows the opposite. Once the occupying forces withdraw from the homeland territory of the terrorists, they often stop—and often on a dime.

In Lebanon, for instance, there were 41 suicide-terrorist attacks from 1982 to 1986, and after the U.S. withdrew its forces, France withdrew its forces, and then Israel withdrew to just that six-mile buffer zone of Lebanon, they virtually ceased. They didn't completely stop, but there was no campaign of suicide terrorism. Once Israel withdrew from the vast bulk of Lebanese territory, the suicide terrorists did not follow Israel to Tel Aviv.

This is also the pattern of the second Intifada with the Palestinians. As Israel is at least promising to withdraw from Palestinian-controlled territory (in addition to some other factors), there has been a decline of that ferocious suicide-terrorist campaign. This is just more evidence that withdrawal of military forces really does diminish the ability of the terrorist leaders to recruit more suicide terrorists.

Once the occupying forces withdraw from the homeland territory of the terrorists, [suicide attacks] often stop—and often on a dime.

That doesn't mean that the existing suicide terrorists will not want to keep going. I am not saying that Osama bin Laden would turn over a new leaf and suddenly vote for George Bush. There will be a tiny number of people who are still committed to the cause, but the real issue is not whether Osama bin Laden exists. It is whether anybody listens to him. That is what needs to come to an end for Americans to be safe from suicide terrorism.

There have been many kinds of non-Islamic suicide terrorists, but have there been Christian suicide terrorists?

Not from Christian groups per se, but in Lebanon in the 1980s, of those suicide attackers, only eight were Islamic fundamentalists. Twenty-seven were Communists and Socialists. Three were Christians.

Has the IRA [Provisional Irish Republican Army] used suicide terrorism?

The IRA did not. There were IRA members willing to commit suicide—the famous hunger strike was in 1981. What is missing in the IRA case is not the willingness to commit suicide, to kill themselves, but the lack of a suicide-terrorist attack where they try to kill others.

If you look at the pattern of violence in the IRA, almost all of the killing is front-loaded to the 1970s and then trails off rather dramatically as you get through the mid-1980s through the 1990s. There is a good reason for that, which is that the British government, starting in the mid-1980s, began to make numerous concessions to the IRA on the basis of its ordinary violence. In fact, there were secret negotiations in the 1980s, which then led to public negotiations, which then led to the Good Friday Accords. If you look at the pattern of the IRA, this is a case where they actually got virtually everything that they wanted through ordinary violence.

The purpose of a suicide-terrorist attack is not to die. It is the kill, to inflict the maximum number of casualties on the target society in order to compel that target society to put pressure on its government to change policy. If the government is already changing policy, then the whole point of suicide terrorism, at least the way it has been used for the last 25 years, doesn't come up.

Are you aware of any different strategic decision made by al-Qaeda to change from attacking American troops or ships stationed at or near the Gulf to attacking American civilians in the United States?

I wish I could say yes because that would then make the people reading this a lot more comfortable. The fact is not only in the case of al-Qaeda, but in suicide-terrorist campaigns in general, we don't see much evidence that suicide-terrorist groups adhere to a norm of attacking military targets in some circumstances and civilians in others.

In fact, we often see that suicide-terrorist groups routinely attack both civilian and military targets, and often the military targets are off-duty policemen who are unsuspecting. They are not really prepared for battle.

The reasons for the target selection of suicide terrorists appear to be much more based on operational rather than normative criteria. They appear to be looking for the targets where they can maximize the number of casualties.

In the case of the West Bank, for instance, there is a pattern where Hamas [a Palestinian militant movement] and Islamic Jihad [a militant movement operating mainly in Uzbekistan] use ordinary guerrilla attacks, not suicide attacks, mainly to attack settlers. They use suicide attacks to penetrate into Israel proper. Over 75 percent of all the suicide attacks in the second Intifada were against Israel proper and only 25 percent on the West Bank itself.

What do you think the chances are of a weapon of mass destruction being used in an American city?

I think it depends not exclusively, but heavily, on how long our combat forces remain in the Persian Gulf. The central motive for anti-American terrorism, suicide terrorism, and catastrophic terrorism is response to foreign occupation, the presence of our troops. The longer our forces stay on the ground in the Arabian Peninsula, the greater the risk of the next 9/11, whether that is a suicide attack, a nuclear attack, or a biological attack.

6

Foreign Occupation Does Not Motivate Suicide Bombers

Scott Atran

Scott Atran is a visiting professor of psychology and public policy at the University of Michigan and director of research in anthropology at France's Centre National de la Recherche Scientifique (CNRS).

The conclusion that suicide bombings are primarily driven by foreign occupation motivation has four critical flaws. First, suicide attacks carried out by secular groups have become rare, while hundreds of the latest can be attributed to self-recruiting Islamic extremists. Second, suicide terrorism today is too broad a phenomenon to draw consistent assumptions about motivations and goals. Third, an organization may resort to suicide bombings to gain visibility and broaden its political base. And, finally, Islamic extremism is gaining ground within unoccupied Muslim areas and populations that have not previously perpetuated such attacks.

Suicide attack is the most virulent and horrifying form of terrorism in the world today. The mere rumor of an impending suicide attack can throw thousands of people into panic. This occurred during a Shi'a procession in Iraq in late August 2005, causing hundreds of deaths. Although suicide attacks account for a minority of all terrorist acts, they are re-

Scott Atran, "The Moral Logic and Growth of Suicide Terrorism," *Washington Quarterly*, vol. 29, no. 2, Spring 2006, pp. 127–134. Copyright © 2006. Reproduced by permission of Taylor & Francis (Routledge).

sponsible for a majority of all terrorism-related casualties, and
the rate of attacks is rising rapidly across the globe. During
2000–2004, there were 472 suicide attacks in 22 countries, killing more than 7,000 and wounding tens of thousands. Most
have been carried out by Islamist groups claiming religious
motivation, also known as jihadis. Rand Corp. vice president
and terrorism analyst Bruce Hoffman has found that 80 percent of suicide attacks since 1968 occurred after the September 11 attacks, with jihadis representing 31 of the 35 responsible groups. More suicide attacks occurred in 2004 than in
any previous year, and 2005 has proven even more deadly,
with attacks in Iraq alone averaging more than one per day,
according to data gathered by the U.S. military. The July 2005
London and Sinai bombings, a second round of bombings at
tourist destinations in Bali in October, coordinated hotel
bombings in Jordan in November, the arrival of suicide bombings in Bangladesh in December, a record year of attacks in
Afghanistan, and daily bombings in Iraq have spurred renewed interest in suicide terrorism, with recent analyses stress-
ing the strategic logic, organizational structure, and rational
calculation involved.

Whereas they once primarily consisted of organized campaigns by militarily weak forces aiming to end the perceived
occupation of their homeland, as argued by University of Chicago political scientist Robert Pape in *Dying to Win: The Strategic Logic of Suicide Terrorism*, suicide attacks today serve as
banner actions for a thoroughly modern, global diaspora inspired by religion and claiming the role of vanguard for a
massive, media-driven transnational political awakening. Living mostly in the diaspora and undeterred by the threat of retaliation against original home populations, jihadis, who are
frequently middle-class, secularly well educated, but often
"born-again" radical Islamists, including converts from Chris-
tianity, embrace apocalyptic visions for humanity's violent salvation. In Muslim countries and across western Europe, bright

and idealistic Muslim youth, even more than the marginalized and dispossessed, internalize the jihadi story, illustrated on satellite television and the Internet with the ubiquitous images of social injustice and political repression with which much of the Muslim world's bulging immigrant and youth populations intimately identifies. From the suburbs of Paris to the jungles of Indonesia, I have interviewed culturally uprooted and politically restless youth who echo a stunningly simplified and decontextualized message of martyrdom for the sake of global jihad as life's noblest cause. They are increasingly as willing and even eager to die as they are to kill.

The policy implications of this change in the motivation, organization, and calculation of suicide terrorism may be as novel as hitherto neglected. Many analysts continue to claim that jihadism caters to the destitute and depraved, the craven and criminal, or those who "hate freedom." Politicians and pundits have asserted that jihadism is nihilistic and immoral, with no real program or humanity. Yet, jihadism is none of these things. Do we really understand the causes of today's suicide terrorism? Do suicide attacks stem mainly from a political cause, such as military occupation? Do they need a strong organization, such as Al Qaeda? What else could be done to turn the rising tide of martyrdom?

Suicide attacks today serve as banner actions for a thoroughly modern, global diaspora inspired by religion and claiming the role of vanguard for a massive, media-driven transnational political awakening.

It's Not Just for Politics Anymore

In *Dying to Win*, Pape claims that foreign occupation is the root cause of suicide terrorism. The rise in attacks correlates with U.S. military occupation of countries whose governments tend to be authoritarian and unresponsive to popular demands. Analyzing data on 315 suicide attacks from 1980 to

2003, he asserts that the common thread linking 95 percent of all suicide attacks around the world is not religion or ideology, but rather a clear, strategic, political objective. They are organized campaigns to compel a modern democracy, principally the United States, to withdraw military forces from a group's perceived homeland. Al Qaeda supposedly fits this model, being driven primarily by the efforts of Osama bin Laden and those sympathetic to his cause to expel the United States from the Arab heartland—Saudi Arabia, Palestine, Egypt, and Iraq—and ultimately from all Muslim countries. On September 11, 2001, for example, 15 of the 19 suicide attackers came from Saudi Arabia, where nearly 5,000 U.S. combat troops were billeted at the time, with 7,000 more stationed elsewhere on the Arabian peninsula.

According to Pape's findings, suicide bombers come disproportionately from among the largely secular and educated middle classes that aspire to freedom and greater opportunities, yet see their hopes stymied by corrupt dictators and one-party elites acting in collusion with U.S. oil and other interests. On the surface, recent trends seem to bolster Pape's thesis. In October 2003, bin Laden warned in a televised video that European nations fighting in Iraq or Afghanistan would be fair game for attack. The next month, suicide bombings targeted the British consulate and HSBC Bank in Istanbul. In December 2003, jihadi Web sites were broadcasting "Iraqi Jihad, Hopes and Risks," a 42-page blueprint for strategically timing bombings to European political events, the first target of which became the March 2004 Spanish elections. (The bombers in these attacks blew themselves up with suicide belts later when cornered by police, and two Madrid plotters who escaped the police dragnet died as suicide bombers in Iraq in April 2005.)

In the last two years [2004 to 2006], suicide attackers have struck in 18 countries, mostly among U.S. allies linked to undemocratic regimes, such as Pakistan, Saudi Arabia, Uzbekistan, and Egypt, or in places with perceived occupations, such as the Palestinian territories, Chechnya, Kashmir, Afghanistan, and Iraq. In Iraq in 2004, there were more suicide attacks than in the entire world in any previous year of contemporary history, involving "martyrs" from 14 other Arab countries, as well as volunteers from all over Europe. Nevertheless, Pape's basic data, correlations, and conclusions about the causes of terrorism are problematic, outdated in the wake of the September 11 attacks, and sometimes deeply misleading.

There also appear to be clear and profound differences between secular nationalist groups . . . who fight to expel occupiers from their homeland, and global jihadis, who fight against perceived global domination.

In broad terms, statistical regularity or predictability alone can only indicate correlations but never demonstrates cause. This study relies exclusively on the computation of statistical trends rather than complementing them with judgments gleaned from nonrandom interviews with the human subjects of study themselves. This dichotomy is unnecessary and even pernicious. Although one should not make the reciprocal mistake of taking personal accounts at face value, structured psychological interviews and systematic observations by anthropologists and other social scientists who participate in the lives of their informants can provide new and surprising alternatives to frame the collection of statistical data. More specifically, at least four critical flaws are embedded in the conclusions drawn from the data.

A Concern with Sampling

First, there is a concern with sampling. Pape continues to argue that "the leading instigator of suicide attacks is the Tamil Tigers in Sri Lanka, a Marxist-Leninist group whose members are from Hindu families but who are adamantly opposed to religion." Yet, in the last three years, the Tigers and the other main secular and nationalist groups in Pape's sample, such as Turkey's Kurdistan Worker's Party (PKK), have carried out very few attacks or none at all. The Tigers have carried out only two confirmed suicide attacks since the beginning of 2002. Although they perhaps remain the leading single organizer of suicide attacks (77 in total), there have been more suicide attacks by various Iraqi groups in 2005 (where more than 400 attacks killed more than 2,000 people) than in the entire history of the Tigers. The Iraqi attacks have not been carried out through a particularly well-organized strategic operation, but rather via a loose, ad hoc constellation of many small bands that act on their own or come together for a single attack. There also appear to be clear and profound differences between secular nationalist groups such as the Tamil Tigers, who fight to expel occupiers from their homeland, and global jihadis, who fight against perceived global domination. For example, Tamil suicide operatives are actively selected by recruiters and cannot withdraw from planned operations without fear of retaliation against their families, whereas the martyrs of the Al Qaeda network are mostly self-recruiting and deeply committed to global ideology through strong network ties of friendship and kinship so that events anywhere in jihad's planetary theater may directly impact actions anywhere else.

Too Narrow and Too Broad

Second, Pape's conclusions about suicide terrorism are both too narrow and too broad. On the narrow side, none of Pape's data indicate that conventional tactics are less useful than suicide attacks in cases where terrorists appear to have scored successes in liberating their homeland. For example, Israel exited southern Lebanon 14 years after Hizballah ceased to use suicide tactics, and the United States withdrew from Somalia after casualties suffered under conventional attack. The category of suicide terrorism today also proves to be too broad and motley a category to draw reliable conclusions about motivations and goals. For example, although the Tigers deserve their due in any inquiry on contemporary suicide terrorism, their relevance to the global diffusion of martyrdom operations is questionable.

Marc Sageman, a forensic psychiatrist and former intelligence case officer, has traced the links among more than 400 jihadis with ties to Al Qaeda. No significant demographic differences emerge between Sageman's global jihadi sample and Pape's more restricted sample of 71 terrorists who killed themselves between 1995 and 2004 in attacks sponsored or inspired by Al Qaeda. In other words, there seem to be no reliable differences between jihadi martyrs in particular and jihadis who fight in the name of global jihad more generally.

Political Market Share

Third, rather than judging as Pape does the success of suicide tactics primarily by whether the sponsoring organization has helped to expel foreigners from its homeland, the broader strategic goal that suicide attacks seek may be to increase the sponsoring organization's political "market share" among its own potential supporters, that is, to broaden its political base among the population and narrow popular support for rival organizations. For example, the Hamas campaign of suicide bombings actually caused Israel to reoccupy Palestinian lands during the second intifada and not to withdraw, but levels of popular support for Hamas increased to rival and at times even surpass support for the Fatah-dominated Palestinian Liberation Organization. Inciting the withdrawal of foreign forces is only one means of accomplishing that goal. Thus, the net effect of the suicide attacks was not to expel foreign forces but to increase the appeal of Hamas. Similarly, the net result of the September 11 attacks was substantially greater U.S. and foreign intervention in Muslim territories, although Al Qaeda's profile rose to the top of the global jihadi ranks.

An Unfounded Inference

Fourth, Pape's argument that suicide terrorism is unrelated or only marginally related to Salafi ideology employs an unfounded inference. Salafis believe that the *hadith* (oral traditions) and literal readings of the Qur'an are sufficient guides for social law and personal life. The most militant among them, the jihadis, believe that all contemporary majority-Muslim countries with the exception of Afghanistan under the Taliban have strayed from the true path of Islam and that the only way back is through violent jihad. Pape relies on statistics to show that "the presence of [U.S.] military forces for combat operations on the homeland of suicide terrorists is stronger than Islamic fundamentalism in predicting" whether someone will become an Al Qaeda suicide terrorist. According to Pape's analysis, nearly one-third of Pakistan's 150 million people are estimated to be Salafi, but the country has produced only two suicide terrorists, whereas Morocco has no Salafis, according to a single secondary source from 1993, but has produced 12 suicide terrorists.

Some of these statistics can be contested, whereas others need to be updated. For example, although Salafism may still lack wide popular support in Morocco, its appeal has grown steadily among the discontented in that country since the 1970s and especially after the return of the Afghan alumni in the 1990s. By the end of 2004, Pakistan had at least 10 suicide bombers in the country, apart from the dozens of suicide terrorists from Pakistan's Kashmiri groups that profess allegiance to global jihad. Similarly, the number of suicide terrorists in heavily Salafi Egypt has quadrupled over the figure presented in Pape's 2003 tables and has more than doubled in Indonesia. Uzbekistan, which had six suicide bombers in 2004 and which Pape listed as having no Salafi population, in fact has large numbers of mostly urban youth who now sympathize with Hizb ut-Tahrir, a radical Islamist movement largely unknown in Central Asia before the mid-1990s, whose proclaimed goal is jihad against the United States and the overthrow of existing political regimes and their replacement with a caliphate run on Salafi principles.

> *The net result of the September 11 attacks was substantially greater U.S. and foreign intervention in Muslim territories, although Al Qaeda's profile rose to the top of the global jihadi ranks.*

As a causal variable, however, "Salafi population in country of origin" is largely irrelevant to what is happening in the world today. Even if the sample's statistical reliability were to hold up for the years that Pape surveyed, suicide terrorism is a rapidly moving phenomenon that still involves relatively small numbers, the significance of which can shift dramatically in a relatively short period of time. Indeed, there were more suicide attacks in the last two years, roughly 600, than in Pape's entire sample between 1980 and 2003. The British-born bombers who attacked London in 2005 or the Malaysians who likely planned the latest Bali bombing belong to the fringe of a large and growing Muslim diaspora.

The Changing Jihadi Landscape

This changing jihadi landscape is revealed in the formation of the cell responsible for the 2004 Madrid train bombings. As early as October 2002, the substitute imam of the Takoua Mosque in Madrid was informing Spanish police under the codename "Cartagena" that a band of friends, unhappy with the mosque's seemingly moderate preachings, had begun calling themselves Al Haraka Salafiya (The Salafi Movement). According to Cartagena, they met "clandestinely, with no regularity or fixed place, by oral agreement and without any schedule, though usually on Fridays." Soon, the informal group of mostly homesick Moroccan descendants and émigrés "reached the conclusion that they had to undertake jihad." By November 2002, opinion within the group began to shift against "going to other countries to undertake jihad, when operations were possible in Morocco and Spain." A detailed action plan only began to coalesce later the following year, however, around the time the Internet tract "Iraqi Jihad, Hopes and Risks" began to circulate a call for "two or three attacks ... to exploit the coming general elections in Spain in March 2004" on the Global Islamic Media Front Web site, to which the Madrid plotters had been systematically logging on since the spring of 2003. The police reports show that targeting trains to force Spain out of the coalition in Iraq was only a late goal emanating from an informal network dedicated to the simple but diffuse project of undertaking jihad to defend and advance a Salafist vision of Islam.

When Egyptian Bedouin are dying to kill European tourists and the Egyptians who cater to them; when British citizens blow themselves up along with other British because of the country's involvement in Iraq and Afghanistan; when jihadis exclusively target co-religionists linked to the secular government in Bangladesh, which is not a particularly close friend of the United States or its allies; when Malaysian bombers kill Australians and Balinese Hindus in Indonesia as "self-defense" in a "clash of civilizations" between Islam and the United States; and when Arabs from more than a dozen countries rush to embrace death in Iraq in order to kill Shi'as, who are probably more supportive of Iran than they are of the United States, it is quite a stretch to identify the common thread as a secular struggle over foreign occupation of a homeland, unless "secular" covers transcendent ideologies, "foreign occupation" includes tourism, and "homeland" expands to at least three continents.

7

Social Factors and Group Membership Influence Suicide Bombers

Paul Gill

Paul Gill is a lecturer at the School of Politics and International Relations, University College Dublin, in Dublin, Ireland.

Although young Muslim males have committed most of the suicide bombings familiar to the United States, Great Britain, and their allies, perpetrators worldwide do not fit a profile and represent a range of religious, gender, racial, and socioeconomic backgrounds. Consequently, it is more useful to examine the path that leads an individual to become an Islamic suicide bomber. This path involves four key stages: exposure to radical Islamic propaganda and alienation from wider society; religious, personal, or political catalysts (e.g. suffering, bereavement); pre-existing social or family ties to extremists; and self-identification, membership, and conformity in extremist groups.

I'm a white, 62-year-old, 6-foot-4-inch suit wearing ex-cop. I fly often, but do I really fit the profile of a suicide bomber? Does the young mum with three tots? The gay couple, the rugby team, the middle aged businessman? . . . The truth is Islamic terrorism in the West has been universally carried out by young Muslim men, usually of ethnic appearance.

Paul Gill, "Suicide Bomber Pathways Among Islamic Militants," *Policing*, vol. 2, no. 4, 2008, pp. 412–419. Copyright © 2008 Paul Gill. All rights reserved. Reproduced by permission Oxford University Press and the author.

The above quote, from an esteemed former member of the Metropolitan Police Service, contains many implications and drawbacks. It assumes that a perfect racial or ethnic profile of a suicide bomber exists based on our familiarity of past perpetrators. Creating a perfect profile is near impossible. Worldwide, suicide bombers have ranged from 15 to 70 years old, been very well educated and uneducated, male and female, and from all socioeconomic classes, Christian, Hindu, Sikh and Muslim, religious and secular, single and married, white and black. Although the majority of suicide bombers the West has experienced, in either its own territory or in Afghanistan or Iraq, are male Muslims under the age of 35, there is nothing to suggest that the Tamil, Chechen, Kashmiri or Palestinian militant movements will never start a campaign of violence in lands foreign to their struggle. This article seeks to move away from the overly deterministic approach of profiling and instead offers a pathway model. This model encompasses the structural and situational processes facilitating and encouraging recruitment of suicide bombers. Illustrative examples drawn upon primarily come from suicide bombers who have committed their bombing against a state within which no widespread conflict is evident, or suicide bombers who left their state of birth to commit a suicide bombing in another state. . . .

The model highlights the contribution of both societal and smaller-group socialization processes to the trajectory of the individual to becoming a suicide bomber. The model proposes that individuals experience four key stages on their path to a suicide bombing: broad socialization processes and exposure to propaganda; experience of catalysts; pre-existing familial or friendship ties and finally in-group radicalization. These four stages are pre-requisites that all suicide bombers experience. The order with which differing suicide bombers experience these stages changes from bomber to bomber. Together, the stages mutually reinforce one another. This paper outlines one such pathway. Firstly, socialization into society or a sub-group within society that supports violence predisposes the individual towards participating in violence. Experiencing a catalyst (which can take many forms) acts as prime motivation to join a militant organization. Pre-existing social or familial bonds facilitate the recruitment process. Finally, the individual radicalizes within the group/cell. The chance of progression from one stage to the next reduces due to structural or personal constraints and hence, overcomes the problem of differential recruitment that the profiling approach suffers from.

Socialization and Other Environmental Factors

Propaganda and proclamations from legitimately perceived leaders supporting suicide bombing help create a pool of willing recruits by enhancing the status of previous militants. Propaganda framing suicide bombers as [celebrities] plays a large role in helping others to choose the same path. Compelling sociological evidence suggests that 'suicidal contagion' exists following an extensively publicized celebrity suicide. Investigations into events such as 9/11, 7/7 [the 2005 London bombings], 21/7 [the 2005 attempted London bombings] and the Madrid bombings consistently reveal a plethora of jihadist propaganda evident in the dwellings and on the computers of the bombers. Evidence also suggests that suicide bomber cells regularly convene to watch videos of atrocities committed against Muslims in Bosnia, Iraq and elsewhere, as well as videos celebrating violence by militant Muslims. One of the 7/7 bombers, Hasib Hussain, was open in school about his support and reverence for the 9/11 bombers. Newspaper reports suggest that two of the 7/7 bombers were present at a party celebrating 9/11 in Beeston, Leeds. Police found pictures of the four 7/7 bombers and Mohammed Siddique Khan's last will and testament in a house belonging to one individual charged over the transatlantic airplane plot.

Other environmental factors facilitating a potentially large pool of recruits include a sense of relative deprivation and collective sense of frustration. These types of environmental factors may predispose individuals within certain communities towards the latter stages of the pathway model outlined later in this paper. For example, experiencing relative deprivation may lead the individual to discourses such as radical Islam that try to explain it and provide repertoires of action to overcome it. This may lead the individual to become socialized with radicalized groups and later recruited into militancy. The strength of in-group attachment provides an antidote to the sense of alienation from wider society. . . .

Propaganda framing suicide bombers as [celebrities] plays a large role in helping others to choose the same path.

Catalysts

Empirical research on terrorists highlights the importance of catalysts to propel individuals to join terrorist groups. Examples include studies of left-wing German and Italian militants, the Red Army Faction and the Ulster Defence Association, the Palestinian factions and various Colombian groups. All provide examples of instances where motivation to join a group is longstanding and mainly influenced by social learning processes but only after a catalyst occurs does motivation to join become salient.

Catalysts can be religious, political or personal in nature. Religious catalysts produce bombers who are more proactive rather than being reactive to political or personal events. Religious catalysts encompass suicide bombers who experience religious radicalization without previous personal suffering or past criminal or deviant behaviour. They are important for many reasons. Religious radicalization often provides the individual a discourse with which to understand the surrounding political environment as well as a script to follow in order to overcome perceived injustices. Religious radicalization often leads to interaction with new networks such as prayer groups. Prominent or charismatic leaders of these networks have the potential to steer members of the group towards more radicalized interpretations of holy texts, the problems of the West and, finally, militancy. . . .

Direct personal suffering because of the surrounding conflict characterizes personal catalysts for suicide bombers from conflict zones such as Palestine, Chechnya and Sri Lanka. The extent and nature of these conflicts differ greatly from the examples studied here and hence personal catalysts take on a different nature. For example, many al-Qaeda inspired or sponsored bombers experience a sense of alienation and/or relative deprivation living in the West. Abdelhalim Badjoudj, an Algerian, apparently became alienated in France, experiencing bigotry and a lack of job opportunities before leaving for Iraq and a suicide bombing. Others feel a sense of vicarious suffering from conflicts in foreign lands through personal contacts. A Shia death squad [in Iraq had] recently killed a close friend of one of the Glasgow Airport suicide bombers. . . . Some do experience personal suffering themselves and later become . . . suicide [bombers]. In April 2008, a former inmate of Guantanamo Bay became a suicide bomber in Mosul, Iraq. Many find themselves wanted by state forces for previous militant activities and become . . . suicide bomber[s] feeling they had no other option. Ihab Youssri Yassin, a suicide bomber in Cairo in April 2005, was wanted along with two others for planning a separate suicide bombing in Cairo three weeks earlier. When the other two accomplices were arrested, Ihab became a suicide bomber. . . .

Political catalysts are more general and cause more altruistic motivations to become a suicide bomber than the previous two outlined. For al-Qaeda-inspired and -supported suicide bombers, political catalysts are usually a feeling of suffering vicariously through the suffering of Muslims worldwide. For example, Idris Bazis left his role as a building surveyor in Manchester and followed the path of jihad [after] the deaths of Muslims in the Balkans. During Shehzaad Tanweer's trip to Pakistan in 2003 'he boasted to family that he wanted to die in a "revenge attack" to express his rage at the way Muslims are treated'. . . .

Direct personal suffering because of the surrounding conflict characterizes personal catalysts for suicide bombers from conflict zones such as Palestine, Chechnya and Sri Lanka.

Pre-existing Social Ties

Motivation to join a militant organization or group is rarely enough to become a member. Instead, recruitment is largely based on familial and friendship ties and on a gradualization basis. Familial ties aid recruitment in the IRA [Provisional Irish Republican Army] and the recruitment of female ETA [Basque Homeland and Freedom] members. Friendship ties are important to Italian and German left-wing militants. Mixtures of both are important to the recruitment process of Palestinian and Colombian groups. . . .

My research highlights that these same pre-existing ties are also essential in the recruitment process of suicide bombers. Illustrative examples of familial ties include Nizar Nawar's uncle who recruited him for an al-Qaeda suicide bombing in Tunisia in April 2002. The brother of an Algerian suicide bomber in Iraq was arrested along with 19 others in Spain for recruiting suicide bombers. Brothers of two of the failed 21/7 bombers are facing trial for aiding and abetting the plot. One of the Madrid bombers' brother[s] was a member of the Algerian terrorist organization, the GIA [Armed Islamic Group]. A second Madrid bomber was the brother-in-law of the leader of the terrorist group Salafia Jihadia. Brothers Abu Abdullah and Abu Harith al-Dousari, from Saudi Arabia, both became suicide bombers in Iraq. Twin sisters Imane and Sanae Laghriss were arrested in Morocco for planning suicide bombings. A husband and wife attempted a suicide bombing in a hotel in Jordan in 2005. The wife's three brothers were killed fighting US forces in Falluja—one of whom was a top aide to al-Zarqawi. A Belgian female suicide bomber in Iraq joined the insurgency with her husband. Friendship bonds are also apparent in many cases. For example, Abdelhalim Badjoudj, a French citizen who carried out a suicide bombing in Baghdad in October 2004, left for Iraq with six friends. The 7/7 bombers met through mutual acquaintances and through participating in the same gym and cricket club. A would-be-bomber in the Iraqi insurgency claimed that he had 15 friends who blew themselves up. The 9/11 hijackers consisted of many pre-existing friendship ties, two sets of brothers and three hijackers who shared tribal affiliations. The Madrid bombers consisted of one set of brothers and many sets of pre-existing friendship ties. . . .

In-group Radicalization

Munir al-Makdah, a trainer of Palestinian suicide bombers, outlines,

> much of the work is already done by the suffering these people have been subject to . . . Only 10% comes from me. The suffering and living away from their land has given the person 90% of what he needs to become a martyr. All we do is provide guidance and help strengthen his faith and help set the objectives for him.

This section deals with the extra 10% that al-Makdah refers to.

Social identity theory (SIT) is an important strand of social psychological thought. Social contexts, the acquisition of group norms and other group processes, SIT argues, influence behaviour rather than rational investigations of costs incurred and benefits accrued. Social identifies derive from perceptions of group membership and the affective importance attributed to membership. In other words, social identifies are 'self-definition in terms of group membership'. SIT argues that individuals seek increased self-esteem from their social identity. From this idea, self-categorization theory predicts that a salient social identity shapes behaviour in terms of perception, attitudes, stereotyping and social comparison. It follows that individuals are more likely to share trust and confidence and be influenced by others who share the same social identity.

SIT accounts for two dual processes: categorization and social comparison. Both processes have their own underlying motivations: to feel positive about oneself and to reduce the complexity of the surrounding world. Group membership redefines individual identity. An internalized group identity coupled with the group holding comparative prestige imbues individual group members with positive social identities. The improvement of self-esteem in the group setting strengthens the individual's group identification. Positive social identities derive from inter-group comparison on grounds that positively affirm high status upon the group one is a member of.

Using multiple bombers at the same time builds more pressure to conform.

Group norms deepen group bonds by increasing group solidarity and aiding the internalization of a group identity. When this occurs, the individual views the newly acquired norms as normal and therefore legitimate. Significant others and group norm acquisition ultimately facilitate the suicide bomber throughout his training, the final process of which is the willingness to sacrifice oneself for the beliefs and norms internalized.

Within a group of significant others who share the same norms, conversation plays a key role. The more they converse on the subject at hand, the more casual and taken for granted the intended action becomes. Many examples exist of groups of suicide bombers withdrawing from their families and immersing themselves within the group. The Hamburg Group lived in an apartment together. The perpetrators of the Madrid bombings hid in a flat on the outskirts of Madrid following the bombings. When police tracked them down, they committed a mass suicide bombing in the flat. The 7/7 bombers withdrew from society into what was later dubbed the 'al-Qaeda gym' in Beeston, Leeds. One of the bombers, Germaine [Lindsay], reportedly '[began] disappearing for days at a time' in the buildup to the bombing. Failed 21/7 bomber Muktar Said Ibrahim also had no contact with his family for over a decade. Germaine [Lindsay's] attempts 'to convert peers often led to confrontations and, over time, it seems Lindsay withdrew from his former friends and adopted a more isolated existence'. Two of the failed 21/7 bombers shared a flat in London together. The Bali bombers from October 2002 radicalized together, isolated from the rest of their small Indonesian village.

Using multiple bombers at the same time builds more pressure to conform. Al-Qaeda and Iraqi insurgents regularly use more than one bomber. The soon-to-be bombers are sent down a path-dependent process whereby the committal of the first individual to a suicide bombing creates pressure on the next to conform and so on. Hasib Hussain, the Tavistock square bomber on 7/7, provides an insight here. Failing to get on the Tube, he rang his three comrades. He received no answer, but left messages: 'I can't get on the Tube [subway train], what should I do?' His comrades had obviously committed their suicide bombings and this placed a responsibility on Hasib to conform and not renege on his task. . . .

The final process within the group for the soon-to-be-bomber is the writing of a last will and testament. This is a future public declaration of the intentions and last thoughts of the individual. Several recurring themes emerge within these last will and testaments, all of which play a role in guarding against the individual opting out of his/her suicide bombing.

8

Sexual Repression Motivates Suicide Bombers

Jonathan Curiel

Jonathan Curiel is a staff writer for the San Francisco Chronicle.

A documentary about Palestinians who failed to carry out suicide bombings exposes their sexual frustration as a source of homicidal rage. In numerous interviews, these individuals claim to be retaliating against the invasion of Israel and its sexualized, permissive culture. However, they were also excited by the prospect of paradise and the seventy-two virgins awaiting them in the afterlife, an alleged promise to martyrs in Islamic theology. Thus, while Israeli occupation is part of the problem, these would-be suicide bombers' perceived lack of power is connected to their repressed sexuality in an impure world.

A feature film about Palestinian suicide bombers called "Paradise Now" caused an outcry earlier this year among Israelis. They said it was too sympathetic toward its main characters, who are depicted as being motivated by anger at Israel's occupation of the West Bank and Gaza.

A new documentary, "Suicide Killers," by French-Jewish filmmaker Pierre Rehov is sure to draw barbs from the other camp. Rehov interviews Palestinians imprisoned for trying to detonate suicide bombs and concludes they're influenced by a religious culture that represses sexual desires and channels the resulting frustration into homicidal rage.

Jonathan Curiel, "The Mind of a Suicide Bomber," *San Francisco Chronicle*, October 22, 2006. Copyright © 2006 Hearst Communications Inc. Reproduced by permission.

The Academy of Motion Picture Arts and Sciences, which nominated "Paradise Now" (directed by a Palestinian) for a 2006 best foreign-language film Academy Award, is considering "Suicide Killers" as a 2007 nominee for Best Documentary. The film, which has already screened in New York, will be shown in San Francisco if Academy judges select it as a finalist in the documentary category.

The question of what motivates some Palestinians to strap on explosives and try to kill Israeli citizens has been debated intensively in the past five years, while a string of attacks has resulted in the deaths of 1,000 Israelis.

Some Palestinians say the bombers are fueled by revenge and hopelessness brought on by decades of Israeli occupation, which have choked off the economic and social life of the Palestinian territories, and by Israeli military actions that have killed and wounded thousands of Palestinians. Palestinian legislator Hanan Ashrawi told the BBC in 2002 that suicide bombers are "driven to desperation and anger by the Israeli activities."

Journalist and United Nations official Nasra Hassan, who has done extensive interviews with Palestinian suicide bombers, found that one of their prime goals was to spread fear in the hearts of Israelis. Hamas members told her that suicide bombings were a legitimate tactic against Israeli aggression. Studies by Israeli researchers have found that Palestinian suicide bombers are motivated by many factors, including religion and a desire to avenge the deaths of other Palestinians.

But filmmaker Rehov reaches different conclusions. Several of the young men whom he interviews behind bars say they are eager to reach paradise and the 72 virgins promised by Islamic theology. "Those who blow themselves up get a good bonus from God—they marry 72 virgins," one tells Rehov. (A Hamas cleric told Hassan that the 72 virgins aren't on hand for sexual gratification, however.) One jailed woman talks about wanting to be the "prettiest" among the heavenly virgins.

"Suicide Killers," Rehov says, is "not politically correct." It minimizes the role that Israel's territorial occupation has on Palestinian anger and emphasizes the sexual repression that Rehov says contributes to the bombers' actions. Still, Bassem Eid, a Palestinian-Muslim journalist and human-rights activist in East Jerusalem, praises the movie for exploring the motivations of suicide bombers, saying in a phone interview, "I think suicide bombing is one of the most severe human rights violations."

Rehov has made five previous nonfiction films about Palestinians or the Palestinian territories, including "Holy Land: Christians in Peril." The *Chronicle* interviewed Rehov by phone from his home in Paris. Here are excerpts:

[*The San Francisco Chronicle*]: *Why did you make this film?*

[Pierre Rehov]: I had originally wanted to make a film about the psychology of (Israeli) victims of suicide attacks. I started interviewing victims, but I realized it was going to be a film (of a story that had been told before)—that the victims' lives were completely torn apart. But something struck me: Everyone told me about the last second before the suicide bomber blew himself up—the look and the smile on his face. I was intrigued about how someone can do something so extreme and have a nice smile on his face. I wanted to discover on the individual level what was hiding behind the smile. This is when I shifted.

In the midst of all this, I talked to one of the girls who survived an attack in Haifa. She was a waitress. She was 17. She saw the taxi stop by the cafe where she was working, she saw a guy come in, going straight to her, and opening his shirt and showing dynamite around his belt. He pointed with his finger toward the dynamite and said to her, "Do you know what this is?"

I've studied psychology, and there are a lot of things connected to flashers—they want to destroy innocence. I realized that these guys in the last minute of their lives have this same behavior. This is when I understood there is something really sexual about this extreme act they want to commit. I knew (about the Islamic religious belief) of 72 virgins, and I also knew about how sexual frustration can lead to people becoming serial killers.

Every [captured Palestinian bomber] said that all our behaviors on Earth are impure, and they were trying to reach purity.

Q: *You interview Palestinians in Israeli jails who tried to detonate suicide bombs or who abetted would-be attacks. Only one of them seems to regret what he tried to do. Did this surprise you?*

A: Every single one of them tried to convince me it was the right thing to do for moralistic reasons. These aren't kids who want to do evil. These are kids who want to do good. If they'd been raised in a different world, with different moral values, they would have been just great kids. This is what struck me the most: The result of this brainwashing was kids who were very good people deep inside (were) believing so much that they were doing something great.

Every one of them said that all our behaviors on Earth are impure, and they were trying to reach purity. They said they were "invaded" by Israeli culture. When they turn on the television, they see half-naked dancers. They were offended by that. They wanted me to understand that all this was forbidden on Earth, but if you did something great for God—like blowing yourself up and killing a bunch of innocent Israelis because they are Jews and don't believe the same thing you believe—you end up being forgiven for all of your sins and will go to heaven and find 72 virgins waiting for you.

Q: *Doesn't your film overemphasize the role of religion in the lives of these suicide bombers? Aren't they more motivated by the harsh conditions in the Palestinian territories and feelings of revenge and helplessness? An Israeli study of Palestinian suicide bombers from 2003 says religious fanaticism is just one of many factors.*

A: It's obviously much more complicated than just to say, "They do it because the next minute they wake up in heaven and 72 virgins take care of them." But my theory applies to Palestinians as well as al Qaeda terrorists, who were in strip clubs the night before they blew up the World Trade Center. It can also apply to a kid from London who's in a very religious family . . . yet lives in a city where everything is possible and open to him.

The (Israeli) occupation is, of course, part of the problem; without the occupation, they wouldn't have to deal with the Israeli culture and wouldn't have to deal with the Israeli presence and wouldn't have the sensation of being unpowerful, and it's very much also connected to pride—and pride is connected to sexuality. It's part of your self. It's part of your behavior as a male or a female. You want to prove to the world that your genes are better than other genes, and these genes should be transmitted. All of this is connected. To just say that on the material level that occupation is painful is completely inaccurate.

I travel a lot in Arab countries. Palestinians live much better, even under occupation, than most Arabs do. If you want to talk about real misery in the Muslim world, go to Libya, or go even to the suburbs of Cairo—then you'll see real misery.

Palestinians in the streets of Jenin are complaining about occupation, but they are complaining about it on a cell phone. (Also) the ones who blow themselves up, when they talk about occupation, Tel Aviv is occupation. My film is not a scientific study. I wanted to make a film showing suicide bombers from the inside. I preferred to follow my instinct.

Q: *Did the prisoners you interviewed know you were Jewish, and did this have any [effect] on the way they responded to your questions?*

A. They kind of knew, but for them, I was French before anything else. For them, an American Jew is like an Israeli, and a French Jew is still French, and an Israeli Jew is pure evil. Being French for them meant that I was a friend. (My religion) wasn't important for them.

You'd be surprised—my crew was entirely Israeli except for the translator, who was Israeli Arab. When they were talking to me, they were talking to a French person through an Israeli Arab who was a brother to them. They didn't care or consider about the presence of an Israeli crew, mainly Jews, with a camera filming them.

If you talk to students in Gaza, they talk about the high level of sexual frustration that they have—that it's not possible to have a normal life.

They looked straight into the camera and said, "Well, we want the Jews to disappear." (But after the filming,) I kept in touch with some of the guys. They gave me phone numbers of their families. (The imprisoned Palestinians) said, "Please, if you go back to my village, talk to my uncle." I'm thinking about making another film about the same subject, maybe go back to one of the jails, now that I know them well.

Q: *Bassem Eid praises your film, but I'm sure many Palestinians will say the contentions in "Suicide Killers" are those of a Western, Jewish journalist with a narrow view about Islamic culture and Palestinian motivations.*

A: If you look at the film, I didn't come up with just Occidental analysts going to a blackboard and saying, "Hey, this is how it works." I came up with people from inside the Palestinian territories. Every single one of my suicide bombers talks about it; a woman talks about wanting to be one of the 72 virgins, saying, "I would have been the prettiest of all." If you talk to students in Gaza, they talk about the high level of sexual frustration that they have—that it's not possible to have a normal life.

I would call my film propaganda if I hadn't tried to get the answers from the suicide attackers themselves. In the film, there is very little written from my hand. It's mostly to describe the backgrounds of the suicide killers. I don't step up in the film as a director to try to make people follow what I believe.

Q: *Until you were 9, you were raised in Algeria. Why have you said that Muslim culture is in crisis?*

A. To make it simple, I witnessed the culture for many, many years. I used to go on vacation in Morocco and Tunisia. Lately, I went back to Algeria for the first time in 40 years. I was born in this culture. I was used to being surrounded by Arabs and by Muslims. I feel very comfortable when I'm with them. I have no problem at all. It's a very warm civilization where solidarity is at a very high level. There's a lot of good aspects about Islam.

Unfortunately, what is going on right now is that Islam itself was not capable of going to the 21st century. Islam didn't have its enlightenment, didn't (lead to) new technologies, didn't participate in the modern world. I'm not saying the modern world is good or bad. Islam didn't participate in the modern world for many reasons, one of them being the level of corruption of the (political) leaders in Islam. In order to stay in place, they promoted for decades this theory that the West, especially Israel, is responsible for all the misery of their people.

I don't recognize the Islam of my childhood. I don't recognize the Islam of my vacations 25 years ago to south Morocco, where there is a lot of poverty and where people consider Islam as a very generous and nonviolent religion.

9

Strategic Objectives Motivate Suicide Terrorism

Richard Sale

Richard Sale is Terrorism Correspondent for United Press International.

According to a retired Israeli military official interviewed by Richard Sale, not only are suicide bombings effective at inflicting more deaths than conventional warfare, they are a low-cost way to offset the difference in military might between Israel and Palestine, there is no real defense against them, they have "severely damaged" the economy, and they provide heroes for the cause of the Palestinian enemy. According to this official, the way to deal with suicide bombings is, not to build physical barriers and increase checkpoints, but to remove some Israeli settlements in return for a "renunciation of suicide attacks."

Suicide bombers are by far the most effective weapon the Palestinians have against Israel, and one against which there is no real defense, a retired Israeli military official and expert on Palestinian intelligence told United Press International.

"The suicide bombing campaign has clearly thrown Israel into disarray. It has demoralized its population and has severely damaged Israel's economy," said Gal Luft, a former lieutenant colonel in the Israel Defense Forces.

Luft described the suicide bomb as "the poor-man's smart bomb," and said using it had enabled the Palestinians to move some way toward alleviating the huge military disparity between them and the Israeli army—widely believed to be one of the most effective military machines on the planet.

"It's the only way the Palestinian Authority can attempt to counter Israel's vastly superior fighting ability and military might," Luft said.

Former CIA official and Middle East expert Stan Bedlington agreed, calling the wave of suicide bombings extremely effective.

"Israel's economy has been severely damaged, and its tourism industry has simply collapsed," he said.

But the main selling point of suicide bombing as an instrument of strategy is its effectiveness, he said.

"If you read a lot of Israel's daily press, you hear of empty shopping malls, stores and shops boarded up, deserted streets at night."

The effects on popular morale are everywhere, said Bedlington.

Said Luft: "A suicide bombing is horrible because it can happen any where with no warning. It can turn the most familiar and safe place into a horror of wreckage in an instant."

But the main selling point of suicide bombing as an instrument of strategy is its effectiveness, he said.

Luft said that during the first year of the second intifada, beginning in September 2000, Palestinian militants launched more than 1,500 shooting attacks on Israeli vehicles in the occupied territories, but killed only 75 people.

But the suicide attacks by Islamic extremists that followed that first wave "killed or maimed more Israelis than the mainstream Palestinian organizations had in 8,000 previous attacks," Luft said.

Luft said that now the Palestinian and Islamic organizations view the suicide attack as the one weapon for which the Israelis have no comprehensive defense.

"They will continue to rely on it, because it has brought real results," Luft said.

Although Israel's massive incursion last April badly damaged the Palestinian Authority infrastructure and rooted out some hard-line terrorists, it would not. . .

. . .the attacks. There is always "a new wave to replace them," Luft said.

"Terrorism is not a military problem, but it is Israel's habit to always think that you can use the military to solve anything," he said.

The April Israeli invasion has only "bred more hatred among the Palestinians and that will produce more suicide bombers."

Luft said that now the Palestinian and Islamic organizations view the suicide attack as the one weapon for which the Israelis have no comprehensive defense.

According to U.S. officials, on June 16, Israel began work on construction of a "separation fence" using barriers, sensors, roads and aerial patrols to try and prevent suicide bombing infiltration.

Israel has also broken up the West Bank into eight security zones comprising 120 army checkpoints and 220 military enclaves.

Not only will these measures not work, said Luft, "they act to increase the prestige of the suicide bombers, which already enjoy "heroic stature." His answer? "Hard bargaining. Use carrots to obtain a declaration renunciation of suicide attacks from the Palestinians in exchange for removal of a number of Israeli settlements," he said.

10

Female Suicide Bombers Seek Equality and Dignity

Mia Bloom

Mia Bloom is an assistant professor in the School of Public and International Affairs at the University of Georgia in Athens, Georgia, and author of Dying to Kill: The Allure of Suicide Terror.

A female suicide bomber has several strategic advantages over males. Besides arousing less suspicion, she is less subject to search and can hide explosives inside her body or under the guise of pregnancy, which reduces the chances of detection even further. For the woman herself, becoming a suicide bomber offers the opportunity to advance in a traditional or male-dominated society. Not content with passive or nurturing roles, some female bombers want to prove themselves as equals to men. Others desire to avenge a death, to reclaim family honor, or to gain redemption from the stigma of rape. However, rather than being empowered, these women submit to a twisted role of self-sacrifice that reinforces patriarchal values.

The woman known as Dhanu stood waiting for former Indian Prime Minister Rajiv Gandhi. It was May 21, 1991. She wore thick glasses that obscured her face and [she] clutched a sandalwood garland; the bulge beneath her orange *salwar kameez* (a traditional Hindu dress) bespoke her appar-

Mia Bloom, "Mother. Daughter. Sister. Bomber," *Bulletin of the Atomic Scientists*, vol. 61, no. 6, November–December 2005, pp. 54–62. Copyright © 2005 by the Educational Foundation for Nuclear Science, Chicago, IL 60637. Reproduced by permission of *Bulletin of the Atomic Scientists: The Magazine of Global Security News & Analysis.*

ent pregnancy. As Gandhi strode toward the podium at the political rally where he was to speak, he acknowledged well-wishers lined along the red carpet. He clasped Dhanu's hand, and she respectfully kneeled before him. With her right hand she activated an explosive device strapped to her belly with a denim belt and embedded with 10,000 steel pellets. Gandhi, his assassin, and 16 others were killed.

Later it was revealed that a policewoman had attempted to prevent Dhanu—an assassin allegedly dispatched by the Liberation Tigers of Tamil Eelam (LTTE)—from reaching the prime minister. But Gandhi had intervened, saying something like, "Relax, baby"—quite possibly the last words he ever spoke.

Gandhi may have been blinded by gender, but if so, he was not the first, nor the last. Even the security-conscious United States, post-9/11, failed to include women among an official profile of potential terrorists developed by the Department of Homeland Security to scrutinize visa seekers. Traditionally, women have been perceived as victims of violence rather than as perpetrators. Yet they are now taking a leading role in conflicts by becoming terrorists and, specifically, suicide bombers—using their bodies as human detonators.

The female suicide bomber is a phenomenon that predates the Rajiv Gandhi assassination. The Syrian Socialist National Party (SSNP), a secular, pro-Syrian, Lebanese organization, sent the first such bomber, a 17-year-old Lebanese girl named Sana'a Mehaydali, to blow herself up near an Israeli convoy in Lebanon in 1985. Out of 12 suicide attacks conducted by the SSNP, women took part in five of them. After Lebanon in the 1980s, female bombers spread to other parts of the globe, including Sri Lanka, Turkey, Chechnya, and Israel. Worldwide, approximately 17 groups have started using the tactical innovation of suicide bombing, with women operatives accounting for 15 percent of those attacks. According to terror expert Rohan Gunaratna, almost 30 percent of suicide attackers are women. Most have belonged to secular separatist organizations, such as LTTE and the Kurdistan Workers' Party (PKK). But recent years have witnessed the worrisome emergence of women suicide bombers in religious organizations.

Historically, to the extent that women have been involved in conflict, they have served supporting roles. Their primary contribution to war has been to give birth to fighters and raise them in a revolutionary environment. The advent of women suicide bombers has not so much annulled that identity as . . . transformed it. Even as martyrs, they may be portrayed as the chaste wives and mothers of revolution. When Wafa Idris became the first female Palestinian suicide bomber to strike Israel in January 2002, an Egyptian newspaper eulogized: "The bride of Heaven preferred death to the pleasures of life, so as to convey a powerful message to the Arab nation." Another editorial noted, "From Mary's womb issued a Child who eliminated oppression, while the body of Wafa became shrapnel that eliminated despair and aroused hope."

To complicate the notions of femininity and motherhood, the female bomber's improvised explosive device (IED) is often disguised under her clothing to make it appear as if she is pregnant and thus beyond suspicion or reproach. Police reports in Turkey have emphasized caution approaching Kurdish women who may appear pregnant; several female PKK fighters disguised themselves this way in order to penetrate crowds of people more effectively and to avoid detection, assuming correctly that they would not be frisked or subjected to intense scrutiny. Israel learned this lesson as well. Hanadi Jaradat, a law student from Jenin who killed 19 civilians in a crowded Haifa restaurant in 2003, wore an explosive belt around her waist in order to feign pregnancy.

Moreover, according to a British security source, "The terrorists know there are sensitivities about making intimate body searches of women, particularly Muslim women, and thus you can see why some groups might be planning to use a female suicide bomber. Hiding explosives in an intimate part of the body means even less chance of detection." The report said a woman could conceal up to 12 pounds of plastic explosives inside her body. The detonator and other components, which can be hidden in a watch, cell phone, or electrical device, could easily be taken past security checkpoints.

The use of the least-likely suspect is the most-likely tactical adaptation for a terrorist group under scrutiny. A growing number of insurgent organizations have adopted suicide bombing not only because of its tactical superiority to traditional guerrilla warfare, but also because suicide bombing, especially when perpetrated by women and girls, garners significant media attention both domestically and abroad.

The recruitment of women by insurgent organizations can mobilize greater numbers of operatives by shaming men into participating. This tactic has parallels to right-wing Hindu women who goad men into action through speeches saying, "Don't be a bunch of eunuchs." This point is underscored by the bombers themselves. A propaganda slogan in Chechnya reads: "Women's courage is a disgrace to that of modern men." Before Ayat Akras blew herself up in Israel in April 2002, she taped her martyrdom video and stated, "I am going to fight instead of the sleeping Arab armies who are watching Palestinian girls fighting alone," in an apparent dig at Arab leaders for not being sufficiently proactive or aggressive against the Israeli enemy.

"When women become human bombs, their intent is to make a statement not only in the name of a country, a religion, a leader, but also in the name of their gender."

But why do these women become suicide bombers? The defining characteristics of a suicide bomber, in general, are elusive. Contrary to popular perception, they are not unbalanced sociopaths prone to self-destructive tendencies. Nor are they poor, uneducated religious fanatics. "The profile of a suicide terrorist resembles that of a politically conscious individual who might join a grassroots movement more than it does the stereotypical murderer, religious cult member, or everyday suicide," notes Robert Pape of the University of Chicago.

Additionally, they may feel a sense of alienation from their surrounding societies, or be seeking retribution for humiliation. (Eyad El-Sarraj, the founder and director of the Gaza Community Mental Health Program, has found that Palestinian suicide bombers share childhood traumas—notably, the humiliation of their fathers by Israeli soldiers.) Suicide bombers tend to emerge in societies that extol the virtues of self-sacrifice. And, crucially, suicide bombers rarely act on their own. They are recruited and indoctrinated by organizations that might exploit their desire for a sense of belonging and that may act as surrogate families.

These same characteristics apply to women suicide bombers—albeit through the unique prism of their experiences and status. In Sri Lanka, Mangalika Silva, the coordinator of Women for Peace in Colombo, observes that, "The self-sacrifice of the female bombers is almost an extension of the idea of motherhood in the Tamil culture. In this strongly patriarchal society, Tamil mothers make great sacrifices for their sons on a daily basis; feeding them before themselves or the girl children, serving on them and so on." Anecdotal evidence suggests that many women bombers have been raped or sexually abused either by representatives of the state or by insurgents—thereby contributing to a sense of humiliation and powerlessness, made only worse by stigmatization within their own societies. They may be avenging the loss of a family member or seeking to redeem the family name. And these women, not content to play the designated roles of passive observer or supportive nurturer, may seek to prove to their own societies that they are no less capable than their male counterparts to be vital contributors to the cause. Clara Beyer, a researcher for the International Policy Institute for Counter-Terrorism in Israel, astutely observes that, "When women become human bombs, their intent is to make a statement not only in the name of a country, a religion, a leader, but also in the name of their gender."

Daughters of Revolution

Insurgent and terrorist organizations have long provided women a potential avenue for advancement beyond what their traditional societies could offer. Women in radical secular organizations have engaged in anticolonial and revolutionary struggles in the developing world and elsewhere since the 1960s. They have played vital support roles in the Algerian revolution (1958–1962), the Iranian Revolution (1979), the war in Lebanon (1982), the first Palestinian Intifada (1987–1991), and the Al Aqsa Intifada (since 2000).

Female terrorists have come from all parts of the globe: Italy's Red Brigades, Germany's Baader-Meinhof faction, America's Black Panthers, and the Japanese Red Army—occasionally emerging as leaders. Women have even been on the front lines of combat, demonstrating that their revolutionary and military zeal is no less than that of men. (The Tamil Tigers have units exclusively for women.) There also have been a handful of notorious Palestinian women militants. In 1970, Leila Khaled was caught after attempting to hijack an El Al flight to London. Khaled, as journalist Eileen Macdonald puts it, "shattered a million and one taboos overnight and she revolutionized the thinking of hundreds of other angry young women around the world."

Khaled explained her rationale: "Violence was a way of leveling the patriarchal society through revolutionary zeal— the women would demonstrate that their commitment was no less than those of their brothers, sons, or husbands. Strategically, women are able to gain access to areas where men had greater difficulty because the other side assumed that the women were second-class citizens in their own society—dumb, illiterate perhaps, and incapable of planning an operation."

More recently, the idea of violence empowering women has spread throughout the West Bank and the Gaza Strip. This militant involvement by women has had an extreme effect on the existing norms of Palestinian society, which has long had a cultural set of rules that describe and limit gender roles. These norms have dictated the separation of the sexes and prescribed that women restrict themselves to the private space of the home.

Through violence, however, women have placed themselves on the front lines, in public, alongside men to whom they are not related. This results in a double trajectory for militant women—convincing society of their valid contributions while at the same time reconstructing the normative ideals of their society. "Palestinian women have torn the gender classification out of their birth certificates, declaring that sacrifice for the Palestinian homeland would not be for men alone," declared female columnist Samiya Sa'ad Al Din in the Egyptian newspaper *Al-Akhbar*. "On the contrary, all Palestinian women will write the history of the liberation with their blood, and will become time bombs in the face of the Israeli enemy. They will not settle for being mothers of martyrs."

The first wave of Palestinian women who became *shahidas* (female martyrs) had varied backgrounds: one ambulance worker, one seamstress, two in college, one in high school, one law school graduate, and one mother of two who left relatives stricken and shocked. Some analysts have suggested a shared characteristic among them, that they were misfits or outcasts—young women who found themselves, for various reasons, "in acute emotional distress due to social stigmatization." Journalist Barbara Victor corroborated this hypothesis when she determined that the first four female Palestinian suicide bombers were in situations where the act of martyrdom was seen as their sole chance to reclaim the "family honor" that had been lost by their own actions or the actions of other family members. Allegations abound that the first female Hamas suicide bomber, Reem Riashi, a mother of two, was coerced by both her husband and lover as a way of saving face after an extramarital affair.

Elsewhere in the world, sexual violence against women—and the ensuing social stigma associated with rape in patriarchal societies—appears to be a common motivating factor for suicide attackers. Kurdish women allegedly raped in Turkey by the military have joined the PKK, while Tamil women allegedly raped by the Sinhalese security services and military join the LTTE. Gandhi's assassin, Dhanu, is alleged to have been raped, although this issue remains one of intense debate and controversy. (By some accounts, it was her mother who was raped by Indian peacekeepers who occupied Sri Lanka from 1987 to 1990). According to the Hindu faith, once a woman is sexually violated she cannot get married or have children. Fighting for Tamil freedom might have been seen as the only way for such a woman to redeem herself.

A theological debate rages as to whether women should or could be martyrs.

For Dhanu, the conflict had another personal dimension: The peacekeepers in Sri Lanka had killed her brother, a well-known cadre for the Tamil Tigers. In that regard, she shared an experience common in conflict-ridden societies—the loss of loved ones. Most of the Chechen attacks against Russia in 2004 involved "Black Widows" reportedly wishing to avenge the deaths of family members in Russia's conflict in Chechnya.

Female bombers have participated in more than 18 major attacks since the outbreak of the second Chechen War in 1999 and have developed into an increasingly serious threat since 2000. Previous acts of violence took place in the Northern

Caucasus and were primarily aimed at military targets. They did not aim to kill large numbers of Russian civilians. The attacks by female suicide bombers have reversed these patterns. Imran Yezhiyev, of the Chechen-Russian Friendship Society in Ingushetia, observes: "Suicide attacks were an inevitable response to the 'most crude, the most terrible' crimes Russian forces had committed against Chechen civilians during the war. When Russian soldiers kill children and civilians and demand payment for their return, many in Chechnya are outraged and vow revenge. One woman, Elvira, whose 15-year-old son had been killed by Russian troops who demanded $500 to return his corpse stated, 'Oh, yes, I want to kill them. Kill Russians, kill their children. I want them to know what it is like.'"

Divine Intervention

Islamic leaders initially opposed women's activism and banned women from becoming suicide bombers on their behalf; only a handful of clerics endorsed such operations. The Saudi High Islamic Council gave the go-ahead to women suicide bombers in August 2001, after a 23-year-old Palestinian mother of two was seized by Israeli security as she brought explosives to Tel Aviv's central bus station. Religious leaders in Palestine disagreed, and a theological debate rages as to whether women should or could be martyrs.

Hamas's former spiritual leader, Sheikh Ahmad Yassin, argued that a woman's appropriate role in the conflict was to support the fighters (that is, the men). According to Yassin, "In our Palestinian society, there is a flow of women toward jihad and martyrdom, exactly like the young men. But the woman has uniqueness. Islam sets some restrictions for her, and if she goes out to wage jihad and fight, she must be accompanied by a male chaperon." Sheikh Yassin further rationalized his reservations—not because of *Shariah* (Islamic religious law), but because women martyrs were deemed unnecessary: "At the present stage, we do not need women to bear this burden of jihad and martyrdom. The Islamic Movement cannot accept all the Palestinian males demanding to participate in jihad and in martyrdom operations, because they are so numerous. Our means are limited, and we cannot absorb all those who desire to confront the enemy."

This situation is alarmingly true. Most of the militant organizations in Palestine cannot fill positions for martyrdom operations fast enough. After Wafa Idris blew herself up in downtown Jerusalem in January 2002, Yassin categorically renounced the use of women as suicide bombers or assailants. Yet, sensing the increasing support for women martyrs and bowing to public pressure and demands, Yassin amended his position, saying that a woman waging jihad must be accompanied by a male chaperon "if she is to be gone for a day and a night. If her absence is shorter, she does not need a chaperon." In a second statement, Yassin granted a woman's right to launch a suicide attack alone only if it does not take her more than 24 hours to be away from home—an ironic position, since she would be gone for longer if she succeeded in her mission.

While Yassin pointed out that it was Hamas's armed wing that decided where and when attacks would take place, his comments included quotes from the videotape that Riashi, Hamas's first female bomber, recorded before carrying out her January 2004 attack, about how she hoped her "organs would be scattered in the air and her soul would reach paradise." Yassin added: "The fact that a woman took part for the first time in a Hamas operation marks a significant evolution. . . . The male fighters face many obstacles on their way to operations, and this is a new development in our fight against the enemy. The holy war is an imperative for all Muslim men and women, and this operation proves that the armed resistance will continue until the enemy is driven from our land. This is revenge for all the fatalities sustained by the armed resistance."

Among Islamic groups, the trend toward women suicide bombers appears to be contagious, as religious authorities are making exceptions and finding legal precedent to permit women's participation. Groups affiliated with Al Qaeda have begun to employ women bombers. An indication of this ideological shift was the capture of two young women in Rabat, Morocco, on their way to target a liquor store in a preempted suicide attack. Within weeks of the U.S. invasion of Iraq, on March 29, 2003, two women (one of whom was pregnant) perpetrated suicide attacks against Coalition forces. Al Jazeera television reported on April 4 that the two Iraqi women had videotaped their intentions: "We say to our leader and holy war comrade, the hero commander Saddam Hussein, that you have sisters that you and history will boast about." . . .

Indeed, some see female suicide bombers as a crucial blow against the decadent influences of Western culture—an act of defiance that does not redefine women's traditional roles, but reaffirms them. A columnist in the Jordanian newspaper *Al-Dustour* noted, "The Arab woman has taken her place and her dignity. It is the women's rights activists in the West who robbed women of their right to be human, and viewed them as bodies without souls. . . . Wafa [Idris] did not carry makeup in her suitcase, but enough explosives to fill the enemies with horror. . . . Wasn't it the West that kept demanding that the Eastern woman become equal to the man? Well, this is how we understand equality—this is how the martyr Wafa understood equality."

Yet, the women who seek empowerment and equality by turning themselves into human bombs merely reinforce the inequalities of their societies, rather than confront them and explode the myths from within. Traditional societies have a well-scripted set of rules in which women sacrifice themselves—the ideal of motherhood, in particular, is one of self-denial and self-effacement. The women who choose the role of martyrs do not enhance their status, but give up their sense of self as they contribute to this ultimate, albeit twisted, fulfillment of patriarchal values.

For their part, terrorist groups will continue to find recruits as long as they can offer women a way out of their societies, a chance to participate as full members in the struggle. As such, increasing women's roles in peaceful activities, addressing their needs during times of peace and during conflict, and protecting and promoting their rights cannot be an afterthought in foreign policy. The best way to fight the war on terror is to make the terrorist organizations less appealing—to men and to women.

11

Female and Male Suicide Bombers Share Similar Motives

Lindsay O'Rourke

Lindsay O'Rourke is a political science doctoral student at the University of Chicago.

The rise of female suicide bombings in Iraq has brought their motivations under scrutiny, leading to speculations of male subordination, sexism, and other factors related to gender. On the contrary, the motives and circumstances that compel women and men to become suicide attackers are quite similar. Primarily, they share profound community loyalty and are driven by grievances against their enemies. While some female bombers are motivated by revenge, male bombers are, too, as it is impossible to claim one sex cares more about family or friends. More women are being recruited because of several key advantages: they are less suspicious, better able to conceal bombs, and more likely to create significant media attention.

Four more Iraqi women carried out suicide bombings in Iraq this week [in the summer of 2008], bringing to at least 27 the number of such attacks this year in that country involving female terrorists. Anyone reading the newspapers or watching television has been treated to a flurry of popular misconceptions about the root causes of female suicide terrorism.

Women, we are told, become suicide bombers out of despair, mental illness, religiously mandated subordination to men, frustration with sexual inequality and a host of other factors related specifically to their gender. Indeed, the only thing everyone can agree on is that there is something fundamentally different motivating men and women to become suicide attackers.

The only problem: There is precious little evidence of uniquely feminine motivations [to ones that drive] women's attacks.

I have spent the last few years surveying all known female suicide attacks throughout the world since 1981—incidents in Afghanistan, Israel, Iraq, India, Lebanon, Pakistan, Russia, Somalia, Sri Lanka, Turkey and Uzbekistan. In order to determine these women's motives, I compared the data with a database of all known suicide attacks over that period compiled by the Chicago Project on Suicide Terrorism.

This research led to a clear conclusion: The main motives and circumstances that drive female suicide attackers are quite similar to those that drive men. Still, investigating the dynamics governing female attackers not only helps to correct common misperceptions but also reveals important characteristics about suicide terrorism in general.

Additionally, claims of coercion are largely exaggerated. For instance, the well-publicized claims that two women who killed dozens in blowing up a Baghdad pet market were mentally retarded were later revealed to be unfounded.

No One Demographic Profile

To begin with, there is simply no one demographic profile for female attackers. From the unmarried communists who first adopted suicide terrorism to expel Israeli troops from Lebanon in the 1980s, to the so-called Black Widows of Chechnya who commit suicide attacks after the combat deaths of their husbands, to the longtime adherents of the Liberation Tigers of Tamil Eelam separatist movement in Sri Lanka, the biographies of female suicide attackers reveal a wide variety of personal experiences and ideologies.

Likewise, while stories of young, psychologically disturbed women being coerced into their attacks makes for compelling news (and rightly emphasizes the barbarity of the terrorist organizations), they represent a small minority of cases. For example, female suicide attackers are significantly more likely to be in their mid-20s and older than male attackers.

Additionally, claims of coercion are largely exaggerated. For instance, the well-publicized claims that two women who killed dozens in blowing up a Baghdad pet market were mentally retarded were later revealed to be unfounded.

Blaming Islamic fundamentalism is also wrongheaded. More than 85 percent of female suicide terrorists since 1981 committed their attacks on behalf of secular organizations; many grew up in Christian and Hindu families. Further, Islamist groups commonly discourage and only grudgingly accept female suicide attackers. At the start of the second intifada in 2000, Sheik Ahmed Yassin, the founder of Hamas, claimed: "A woman martyr is problematic for Muslim society. A man who recruits a woman is breaking Islamic law." Hamas actually rejected Darin Abu Eisheh, the second Palestinian female attacker, who carried out her 2002 bombing on behalf of the secular Aqsa Martyrs Brigade.

So, what does motivate female suicide attackers? Surprisingly similar motives driving men to blow themselves up on terrorist missions.

For one, 95 percent of female suicide attacks occurred within the context of a military campaign against foreign occupying forces, suggesting that, at a macro level, the main strategic logic is to create or maintain territorial sovereignty for their ethnic group. Correspondingly, the primary individual motivation for both male and female suicide bombers is a deep loyalty to their community combined with a variety of personal grievances against enemy forces.

Terrorist organizations are well aware of the variety of individual motives for male and female attackers. As such, recruitment tactics aimed specifically at women often involve numerous, even contradictory, arguments: feminist appeals for equal participation, using a suicide attack as a way to redeem a woman's honor for violations of the gender roles of her community, revenge, nationalism and religion—almost any personal motive that does not contradict the main strategic objective of combating a foreign military presence.

Yes, many female suicide terrorists are motivated by revenge for close family members or friends killed by occupation forces. But so too are males.

All secular organizations that employ suicide bombings have used female attackers early and often. For instance, 76 percent of attackers from the Kurdistan Workers' Party in Turkey have been women, as have 66 percent of Chechen separatist groups, 45 percent of the Syrian Socialist National Party's and a quarter of those from the Tamil Tigers.

Religious groups only came to realize the strategic value of female bombers after seeing secular groups' success. For example, in a 2003 interview, a female Al Qaeda agent calling herself Um Osama told a Saudi newspaper that "the idea of women kamikazes came from the success of martyr operations carried out by young Palestinian women in the occupied territories."

The Strategic Appeal

Why use women?

Paradoxically, the strategic appeal of female attacks stems from the rules about women's behavior in the societies where these attacks take place. Given their second-class citizenship in many of these countries, women generate less suspicion and are better able to conceal explosives. Moreover, since female attacks are considered especially shocking, they are more likely to generate significant news media attention for both domestic and foreign audiences.

In a similar vein, my research showed that women were much more likely than men to be used for single-target assassination suicide attacks. Perhaps the most famous of these was the 1991 assassination of India's prime minister, Rajiv Gandhi, by Thenmuli Rajaratnam, a Tamil Tiger. Although women make up roughly 15 percent of the suicide bombers within the groups that employ females, they were responsible for an overwhelming 65 percent of assassinations; one in every five women who committed a suicide attack did so with the purpose of assassinating a specific individual, compared with one in every 25 for the male attackers.

Yes, many female suicide terrorists are motivated by revenge for close family members or friends killed by occupation forces. But so too are males. Indeed, there are so many known instances of personal revenge driving both sexes to strike, and so much missing data about the friendship and extended family circles of suicide attackers, that it is simply impossible to say one sex cares more about others.

So, how can we defend against the spate of female suicide attacks in Iraq? The logical first step is to better screen women at key security checkpoints. Coincidentally, American officials recently started a "Daughters of Iraq" program to train Iraqi women to search for female attackers. However, the program is unlikely to have a substantial effect for three reasons: First, the program is very small; only about 30 women initially graduated from the course, and each is expected to work only a few days a month. Second, since the root cause of suicide terrorism appears to be anger at occupying forces, we risk blowback if we are seen as trying to buy loyalty from Iraqi women. Third, the fact that religious groups changed their position on employing women attackers illustrates their willingness to develop new tactics to overcome security measures—thus efforts like the Daughters of Iraq are probably stopgap measures at best.

In the long run, decreasing female suicide attacks depends upon an American strategy that minimizes the presence of United States troops in what Iraqis consider their private sphere, while simultaneously providing material support that will improve the quality of life for all Iraqis. For now, however, given the strategic desirability of female attackers, we're likely to see an increasing number of Iraqi women killing themselves and their countrymen in an effort to end what they see as the occupation of their nation.

12

Suicide Terrorism Is Not a New Phenomenon

National Counterterrorism Center

National Counterterrorism Center "serves as the primary organization in the United States Government (USG) for integrating and analyzing all intelligence pertaining to counterterrorism (except for information pertaining exclusively to domestic terrorism)."

Depending on the definition of suicide terrorism, different sources cite different incidents as the first examples of the phenomenon. The first modern suicide bombing may have been the attack that took the life of Tsar Alexander II, though the attacker may not have intended to die in the blast. The first true suicide bomber may have been responsible for the Bath, Michigan, attack, but this may not have involved terrorism. One source gives the attack on the Iraqi Embassy in Beirut, Lebanon, on December 15, 1981 as the first true suicide bombing. The first female suicide bomber made her attack in 1985, also in Lebanon.

On 13 March 1881 (NS)[1], near the Winter Palace, St. Petersburg, Russia, an assailant threw an improvised explosive device (IED) under the armored carriage of the Tsar where it exploded, killing one bodyguard, injuring the driver, and several civilian bystanders, and damaging the carriage. The assailant was arrested immediately by other guards. While Tsar Alexander II inspected the site of the explosion, a suicide

National Counterterrorism Center, "Fact Sheet: Did You Know the First Suicide Bombing May Have Occurred in 1881?" December 12, 2007. Document No. 20071212-06. Reproduced by permission.

bomber approached and threw another IED at the Tsar's feet where it exploded, fatally wounding the Tsar and critically injuring 20 others. On the same day at 3:30 PM, the Tsar died from his wounds. Members of the People's Will, a Russian revolutionary organization, were arrested, tried and executed for the assassination.

The second bomb severed one of Alexander's legs and shattered the other.[2] He was taken to the nearby Winter Palace where he bled to death. He was alive long enough to receive communion, and for family to be with him in his last moments.[3] At his side were Alexander III and Nicholas II who would become future Tsars. Scarred by what they had witnessed, it is believed they suppressed civil liberties to prevent befalling the same fate. It was later learned that a third assailant was waiting within the crowd and prepared to detonate a bomb had the first two bombings failed.[4]

Some credit this attack as the first recorded suicide bombing in history. There is no definitive evidence, however, that the assassin intended to give up his own life to kill the Tsar.[5] Others point to the book of Judges (16:30) for the first recorded suicide attack on non-combatants, in which Samson intentionally dies with his victims in the collapse of a Philistine temple.

The first female suicide bomber may have been Sana'a Mehaidli of the Syrian Social Nationalist Party (SSNP) who detonated her car bomb on 9 April 1985, in Lebanon, killing two Israeli soldiers and injuring two others.

According to MIPT[6], the first suicide bombing was on 15 December 1981, in Beirut, Lebanon, at the Iraqi Embassy which claimed the life of the Iraq Ambassador to Lebanon. There was a claim by the Army for the Liberation of Kurdistan; and by the Iraqi Liberation Army – General Command; and also by the al Dawa ("The Call"), a Muslim fundamentalist group. However, the 1927 Bath, Michigan suicide bombing is likely to be the first definitive suicide bomber, although depending on the definition used some might argue it was not "terrorism".

The first female suicide bomber may have been Sana'a Mehaidli of the Syrian Social Nationalist Party (SSNP) who detonated her car bomb on 9 April 1985, in Lebanon, killing two Israeli soldiers and injuring two others. It must be pointed out, however, that her targets were likely considered combatants, which makes her attack insurgency rather than terrorism.

[References]

1. NS refers to the current dating style we use today, vice the old style dating which would make the date 1 March 1881.

2. Graham, Stephen. "Tsar of Freedom: The Life and Reign of Alexander II," Yale University Press, New Haven. 1935.

3. Radzinsky, Edvard. "Alexander II: The Last Great Tsar," Freepress 2005, p. 413

4. "Alexander II of Russia", Wikipedia.com, 12 Dec. 2007

5. Hoffman, Bruce. "Inside Terrorism" Columbia University Press, New York. 1998, pp 17-19.

6. The Oklahoma City National Memorial Institute for the Prevention of Terrorism (MIPT), www.mipt.org

Organizations to Contact

The editors have compiled the following list of organizations concerned with the issues debated in this book. The descriptions are derived from materials provided by the organizations. All have publications or information available for interested readers. The list was compiled on the date of publication of the present volume; the information provided here may change. Be aware that many organizations take several weeks or longer to respond to inquiries, so allow as much time as possible.

American Civil Liberties Union (ACLU)
125 Broad Street, 18th Floor, New York, NY   10004
Web site: www.aclu.org

Founded in 1920, the ACLU is a nonprofit and nonpartisan organization that focuses on basic freedoms. It has more than 500,000 members and supporters, and it handles nearly 6,000 court cases annually from offices in almost every U.S. state. The ACLU addresses issues such as the Iraq war and homeland security, and it publishes a set of handbooks on individual rights.

American Task Force on Palestine (ATFP)
815 Connecticut Ave., Suite 200, Washington, DC   20006
(202) 887-0177 • fax: (202) 887-1920
e-mail: info@atfp.net
Web site: www.americantaskforce.org

ATFP is a nonprofit, nonpartisan organization. It asserts that it is in the American national interest to promote an end to the conflict in the Middle East through a negotiated agreement that provides for two states—Israel and Palestine—living side by side in peace and security. The organization was established in 2003 to provide an independent voice for Palestinian Americans and their supporters and to promote peace. AFTP's board of directors is made up of a large group of noted Palestinian Americans who agree with these principles.

The Center on Terrorism

John Jay College, New York, NY   10019
(212) 237-8433 • fax: (212) 237-8468
e-mail: terrorism@jjay.cuny.edu
Web site: www.jjay.cuny.edu/terrorism

John Jay College of Criminal Justice lost sixty-seven students and alumni in the World Trade Center disaster. That loss, and the increased interest in terrorism on the part of concerned citizens, prompted John Jay College to create the Center on Terrorism in late 2001. The goals of the center are to study terrorism conceptually in ways that are familiar and appropriate for a university, and to identify the practical applications of that knowledge in the search for alternative forms of human security. The center recently launched its John Jay & ARTIS Transnational Terrorism Database.

Institute for National Strategic Studies (INSS)

National Defense University, Fort Lesley J. McNair
Washington, DC   2013-5066
e-mail: berlink@ndu.edu
Web site: www.ndu.edu/inss

INSS is a policy research and applied strategic learning organization within the National Defense University serving the U.S. Department of Defense, its components, and interagency partners. The mission of the institute is to assess the emerging security environment, develop new strategic concepts and integrated strategies to manage complex challenges, and advance strategic thinking for the Secretary of Defense, Chairman of the Joint Chiefs of Staff, Combatant Commanders, and other components of the National Defense University and Joint and Professional Military Education, as well as for the broader security community, including spanning the interagency and key national and international audiences.

Islamic Society of North America (ISNA)
PO Box 38, Plainfield, IN   46168
(317) 839-8157 • fax: (317) 839-1840

For over forty years, ISNA has provided many services to the Muslim community of North America, including the ISNA Annual Convention. In addition to building bridges of under-standing and cooperation within the diverse Islamic Commu-nity in America, ISNA aims to play a pivotal role in extending those bridges to include all people of faith within North America.

Muslim Students Association of the U.S. & Canada (MSA National)
PO Box 1096, Falls Church, VA   22041
(703) 820-7900 • fax: (703) 820-7888
e-mail: manager@msanational.org
Web site: www.msanational.org

Established in January 1963, MSA National continues to serve Muslim students during their college and university careers by facilitating their efforts to establish, maintain, and develop lo-cal MSA chapters. First established on the campus of the Uni-versity of Illinois at Urbana-Champaign by a conference of Muslim students from around the U.S. and Canada, MSA Na-tional has been uniting Muslim students from diverse back-grounds for more than four decades.

U.S. Department of Homeland Security (DHS)
Washington, DC   20528
(202) 282-8000
Web site: www.dhs.gov

The mission of DHS is to prevent terrorist attacks within the United States, reduce America's vulnerability to terrorism, and minimize the damage and recover from attacks that do occur. Although the department was created to secure the country against those who seek to disrupt the American way of life, its charter also includes preparation for and response to all haz-ards and disasters.

Washington Institute for Near East Policy
1828 L Street NW, Suite 1050, Washington, DC   20036
(202) 452-0650 • fax (202) 223-5364
Web site: www.washingtoninstitute.org

Founded in 1985, the Washington Institute for Near East Policy advances a balanced and realistic understanding of American interests in the Middle East. Under the guidance of a distinguished and bipartisan board of advisors, the Institute seeks to bring scholarship to bear on the making of U.S. policy in this vital region of the world. Drawing on the research of its scholars and the experience of policy practitioners, the Institute promotes an American engagement in the Middle East committed to strengthening alliances, nurturing friendships, and promoting security, peace, prosperity, and democracy for the people of the region.

Bibliography

Books

Diego Gambetta   *Making Sense of Suicide Missions.*
New York: Oxford University Press,
2005.

Mohammed   *Suicide Bombers in Iraq: The Strategy*
M. Hafez   *and Ideology of Martyrdom.*
Washington, DC: United States
Institute of Peace Press, 2007.

Lee Harris   *The Suicide of Reason: Radical Islam's*
Threat to the West. New York: Basic
Books, 2007.

R.B. Herath   *Sri Lankan Ethnic Crisis: Towards a*
Resolution. Victoria, BC: Trafford
Publishing, 2006.

Matthew Levitt   *Hamas: Politics, Charity, and*
Terrorism in the Service of Jihad. New
Haven, CT: Yale University Press,
2006.

Omar Nasiri   *Inside the Jihad: My Life with Al*
Qaeda: A Spy's Story. New York: Basic
Books, 2006.

Anne Marie   *The Road to Martyrs' Square: A*
Oliver and Paul   *Journey into the World of the Suicide*
F. Steinberg   *Bomber.* New York: Oxford University
Press, 2006.

Robert Pape — *Dying to Win: The Strategic Logic of Suicide Terrorism*. New York: Random House, 2005.

Ami Pedahzur, ed. — *Root Causes of Suicide Terrorism: The Globalization of Martyrdom*. New York: Routledge, Taylor, & Francis Group, 2006.

Periodicals

Robert Baer — "The Making of a Suicide Bomber," *Sunday Times*, September 3, 2006.

Ted Byfield — "It's the Religion, Stupid: Journalists Will Never Understand the Motives of Suicide Bombers Until They Understand Their Beliefs," *Western Standard*, August 14, 2006.

CIO Insight — "Experts Say West Can't Stop Web Radicalization," November 7, 2007.

Economist — "Just What Are They Dreaming Of?" February 9, 2008.

Harold Evans — "Palestinians Training Kids to Be Suicide Bombers," U.S. *News & World Report Online*, December 19, 2008.

Amin A. Muhammad Gadit — "Suicide Bombers Deconstructed," *Clinical Psychiatry News*, April 2009.

Hekmat Karzai and Seth G. Jones — "How to Curb Rising Suicide Terrorism in Afghanistan," *Christian Science Monitor*, July 18, 2006.

Matt McAllester   "The Faces Of Death," *Details*, September 2008.

Tim McGirk   "Moms And Martyrs," *Time*, May 14, 2007.

Shazia Mirza   "Stand By for the Gay Muslim Suicide Bombers—They're the Ones with Christian Louboutin Briefcases," *New Statesman*, July 19, 2007.

Kevin Peraino   "Destination: Martyrdom," *Newsweek International*, May 12, 2008.

James V. Schall   "Martyrs and Suicide Bombers," *Ignatius Insight*, August 24, 2005.

Shenali Waduge   "Suicide Terrorism: Why Are Sri Lanka's Women Blowing Themselves Up?" *The WIP*, September 22, 2008.

Washington Times   "The Unsettling Lure of Suicide Terrorism," June 18, 2005.

World Net Daily   "Probe Finds Terrorists in U.S. 'Training for War,'" February 17, 2006.

Index